T0196874

LIFE, LOVE
and Raw Emotion

KAYLEE CLINCH

BALBOA.
PRESS

A DIVISION OF HAY HOUSE

For my dearest friend.
Thank you for allowing me to share so
much of your pain in my poems.

Balboa Press books may be ordered through booksellers or by contacting:

Balboa Press
A Division of Hay House
1663 Liberty Drive
Bloomington, IN 47403
www.balboapress.com.au
1 (877) 407-4847

Because of the dynamic nature of the Internet, any web addresses or
links contained in this book may have changed since publication and
may no longer be valid. The views expressed in this work are solely those
of the author and do not necessarily reflect the views of the publisher,
and the publisher hereby disclaims any responsibility for them.

The author of this book does not dispense medical advice or prescribe the use
of any technique as a form of treatment for physical, emotional, or medical
problems without the advice of a physician, either directly or indirectly. The
intent of the author is only to offer information of a general nature to help
you in your quest for emotional and spiritual well-being. In the event you use
any of the information in this book for yourself, which is your constitutional
right, the author and the publisher assume no responsibility for your actions.

Any people depicted in stock imagery provided by Thinkstock are models,
and such images are being used for illustrative purposes only.
Certain stock imagery © Thinkstock.

Print information available on the last page.

ISBN: 978-1-5043-1108-3 (sc)
ISBN: 978-1-5043-1109-0 (e)

Balboa Press rev. date: 10/31/2017

Contents

25Th Anniversary Wishes

They said you'd never make it,
They said you'd never last.
Although Lyn, I know you've said,
Al's been a real pain in the ass.

25 years have come and gone,
what seems in a blink of an eye.
You've achieved a lot in those years,
now you can look back and sigh.

What happened to those early years,
when to be 45 was old?
Now middle age you do not fear,
for your love is never cold.

At just 18 Alan and Lynda,
were joined in harmony.
On a day full of storms and thunder,
and a sky so bleak and cloudy.

25 years down the track,
he's still the love of her life.
And Al I'm sure, doesn't regret,
taking Lyn for a wife.

Please join with me in wishing them,
A happy 25th
For I know you will all agree
Love IS the greatest gift!

A Different Life Is Ahead

A poem I will write, of encouragement for you
Read this every day, it will help you get through.
I hear you say the days are long and work is tough,
You really need to relax, but can't get enough.

Your life has not ended, but has merely changed
Your heart and your head, is a must to re arrange.
Encouragement to change your routine my dear.
Is that what you seek and is it what you fear?

You know others can see you've been a good wife,
As that chapter closes, it is time to seek a new life.
You are entitled to be happy, there is no law
For it's what you deserve, so let's go through that door!

Grip a new handle, hold it firm and yank it open quick!
See?.........it's not that bad, but beware of the pricks.
For many large thorns abound, in this new daily life
They will stab at your happiness with a black hearted knife.

Friends some may claim to be, others are just jealous
Don't listen when they say to stand back, life is too precious!
Don't waste your thoughts, for those who sneer,
It's just your independence, that they want to spear.

Enough of this pain, this suffering this hurt,
Life's not the same yes, we agree, but go on and flirt.
Enjoy your life, for how long we don't know
God makes these decisions, on how old we grow.

You still have so much to give and so much to share,
So spend your hours with those, who really care.
Ignore the people or friends if they are,
Who's trouble they bother you with, have a look from afar.

You'll see for yourself, they know you'll care
They ham it up for you, then leave you bleeding and bare.
Your emotions they've drained, how clever they scheme
That's another day they've claimed, wake up from your dream.

Let go of the anchors, for your wings want to fly
They're weighing you down, they don't want you to try.
A different life with adventure, is all that's ahead
The uncertain I'm sure, is what we all dread.

It's so hard to interpret how living must be done
You can't enjoy your life, measuring it by rule of thumb.
So please get out there and go, no time to waste
There is so much to enjoy, so rush post haste!!

Life's Too Short

I think about times gone by, all those years we let slip by.
Sorry words left unsaid, sleepless nights, laying in bed.
We should have cleared the air, but neither of us would
We'd pretend we didn't care, it hasn't done us any good.

Life's too short and too damn hard
Enough pain, Dad, please let down your guard.
For hear me now, these words I want to say
I LOVE YOU Dad, and I hope you never go away.

But if that is the path, down which you tread
I want you to remember, those 3 little words I said.
I promise I won't judge you, for whatever you do
You will always be my Father, that will always be true.

I want you to just be happy, and never fear
I'll always love you, I'll always be here.
Too many tears, I have cried in the past,
The old ways Dad, they really can't last.

You'll make a new life, somewhere nice for you
Look for the horizon, and take in the view.
I am the horizon, and you are the sky
I'll always be here, I'll never say goodbye.

The horizon changes shape, the sky changes colour
But you never see one, without seeing the other.
Our bond may be twisted, may be buckled and bent
But do not waste, what once was heaven sent.

No matter if one day Dad, we are forced apart
It will never be my wish, just look deep in my heart.
So, don't dwell on times, when I get mad with you
Remember on those days, I'm still your little girl too.

Deep inside us all, there is a very small child
Sometimes uncontrollable, sometimes a little wild.
So, when the little girl inside me, cries and sobs,
She's needing a hug from her Daddy, it's one of his jobs.

Did You Really Care For Me

Our love started out exciting, it was all so sublime.
I was totally captivated by you, it felt like a crime
When I would ask, you said you would be there for eternity,
I was blinded by love, but did you really care for me?

Was I just an ego challenge, another man's wife?
I wonder now if you knew, it would cost a life.
A life so cheap and empty, it mattered to you not.
I didn't realise your love for me, stopped burning hot.

Loving you cost my life, and you don't even care.
I want you to know, I was engulfed with despair.
The years of heartache, worry, tears and pain,
I wanted it to stop, so I boarded that plane.

No one would have known, and I didn't fear,
My thoughts were so muddled, your face I held dear.
I was alone in the darkest place in my mind
One big deep breath, and it's all left behind.

No more tears will fall, no more will I cry,
Just questions I guess, about the last goodbye.
Family ask, "Why did she do it? Was she mad?"
Friends ask, "Was life really, all that bad?"

For me they were, so many days lost in pain
Now I'll never have to go, through those again.
From my peaceful place, I can see you now
Your unforgettable face, your furrowed brow.

You made me feel, I was only for sport.
All fun and games, until we were caught.
When I committed to you, your battle was won
I was naïve to think our journey had just begun.

It appears my passing hasn't caused you grief,
You flash your smile and whisper "Life is too brief".
Incredibly to another lonely girl you are telling lies,
Same ones you told me, while you look in her eyes.

I didn't mean much to you, It's obvious now
As I watch you say "I do", I can hear your vow.
"To love and to cherish, til death do us part"
I can't listen no more, you've ripped out my heart.

My life with you was good but a crazy mess,
Countless times I craved for your soft caress
Too late I realised, the choice was wrong
Your heart no longer played, to my song.

A cloud has come, and lifted me high
Now I have to kiss my dreams goodbye
My soul fades with the beautiful sun
You had me once, but now I'm gone.

Death comes with great relief
My heart won't break, I found my peace.
Goodbye my Prince, I'll let you be
But you'll always mean, so much to me.

I'm So In Love With You

Have you ever known, eyes so sad?
Days full of misery, you just feel bad?
Have you ever felt, so incredibly alone?
And you wish you knew, someone to phone?

Days and weeks are lost, blinded by tears
Is this all in my head, my insecurity fears?
Every day I waste, is a day closer to death
How I wish it sooner, how I wish I could rest.

No one is here for me, no arms to hold
No warmth from a loving body, I feel so cold.
I yearn for you, but I can't believe you sleep!
My body is wracked, from the tears I weep.

My mind is exhausted and numb from the pain
I'm sure I'm doing, Satan's work again.
A lesson is learnt, each and every day
For breaking God's commandments, a price I must pay.

To commit no sin, you must be so pure
But I'm so in love with you, there is no cure.
For a heart to break, it takes no strength
But once it's let down, it won't go the length.

"What's wrong with you?" I hear you say
"You must be crazy, to feel this way!!"
I am crazy. THAT I know for sure
For every day I knock at the Reaper's door.

"Let me in!" I beg and plead each day,
Just to take me and this pain away.
I ask myself what will I leave behind?
There is nothing I can see, that will mind.

Life without me here will remain the same
Comments of "She's gone? Oh, what a shame"
It really seems no one cares, I'm so depressed
So many tears that fall, down on to my dress.

There's only me here, to wipe them dry
Some days it just feels better, to have a good cry
I've tried to explain but never will you understand
You shut me down and refuse to take my hand.

I've asked you to walk with me, in my shoes,
Open your eyes to see how I get the blues.
I give you so much love, that's sent one way
I'm hoping for it to return, one day.

I have so much more to give, to offer you
Why can't you see, what it is you do?
I'm dying inside, I am a real mess
I'm so screwed up, I can't even guess.

What goes on behind your eyes?
And why do you tell me, so many lies?
I can't take no more, I just want to run
Where is somebody, when you need some fun?

I don't know if I matter, but what if I did?
Where are you now??? Asleep in our bed??
I want to scream, but don't know if I can
How would you react? Would you be a man?

Would your heart fall apart? When you look in my eyes?
And feel the heartache, from these tears that I cry?
Why can't you hear me?? Why do you dream??
Why don't you know, your name I could scream??

Please acknowledge, the love I am sending
It used to be so good, back in the beginning.
Wake up you fool!! Look, listen and see!!
I don't know what's happening, inside of me.

Memory Lane

Come on a trip down memory lane, that time has forgotten
Trust me, take my hand, It's not all that rotten.
Our history goes back, way way back in time
When I was so young and you were nearly nine.

I've loved you forever, in fact all my life
Even when I became, another man's wife.
We leaned on each other, our childhood was tough,
And when we played together, we played pretty rough.

We worked for pocket money, it wasn't a lot
We'd have nothing left, we'd spend all that we got.
We earnt 20 cents each and you'd take mine from me
And feed it in the Pin Ball Machine, I could barely see.

I didn't mind though, I thought you were great
You made all the lights flash, and you were only eight.
We'd catch the school bus, our eyes would not meet
And heaven help me, if I came near your seat.

To say my surname at school, you thought it a crime
You wanted no one to know, about our bloodline.
I busted you big time, showing Lee how you drive
If your parents found out, they'd have skinned you alive.

The backyard pool, we didn't swim in it much
Someone put a shovel through it, in a finishing touch.
Cigarettes were forbidden, yes they were taboo
And didn't you panic, when your Dad busted you?

Yes those days are over, I'm not sorry for that
You were ever so cruel, to my precious pet cat.
You would drop kick her, with a roar and a cheer
"10 points" you'd say, if the fence you could clear.

You made tuna sandwiches, because I was in a "mood"
Lucky we didn't eat them, as it was the cat's food!
You blamed Old Billy, for beer cans behind the shed
When your Dad found them, he believed every word you said.

Sport was your life, then you broke you jaw
No more football for you, just hamburgers through a straw.
You loved your sport, and played them so well
We watched you play cricket, and football was hell.

Your mother she would scream, "get off his head"
All I wanted to do, was crawl back to my bed.
Big Brother on guard, you stood up for your sis
You showed a guy the door, for stealing a kiss.

Life drew us apart, and fate drew us together
Who ever thought, we'd live streets from each other?
Your boys are sports mad, they'll grow up like you
And break the girls hearts, as footy players do.

Well the trip is over, was it that bad?
Two children now grown up, old age is sad.
Yes, you are my hero, I'm not ashamed to admit
You're strong and brave, and I love every bit.

What Would You Know?

You remind me of someone, I once thought I knew,
But listen to you talk, you're always so blue.
I'm nothing like that, I'm a happy little bee,
I'm so smiley and bouncy, people just love me.

You spend your hours, deep in miserable thought,
And anguish over the years, and the memories they brought
You cry and you sob, and you try to forget,
The things you've done, they bring you regret.

People don't like you, they don't come near
Your eyes always puffy, your face wet with tears.
You're painful and ugly, your world is all black,
If I saw you in the street, I'd just turn my back.

I don't need someone like you, my life is perfect and clear
I'm at my happiest, without you near.
And listen to you now, you scoff and mock
My happiness you say, is a whole lot of crock.

ENOUGH!!! I hear what you say! I think it's you that needs to look,
And stop living in a dream, or your fairy tale book!
You dare to judge me, to scorn and hurt,
You're nothing but a phoney and a ridiculous flirt.

Here's some of my advice, take a leaf from MY book,
The way you are, is not how you look
Look in the mirror, and tell me what you can see.
Surprised you, did I? because you ARE me!!

Thank You My Friend

We met via email
Linked by a job
Our lives are so busy
Oh, the times we could sob.

Our friendship developed,
As most friendships do
We found out interests
That we could relate to.

The miles separate us
The ocean our enemy
Still our hearts are warmed
For that chance meeting to be.

I'd love to give you a hug
You've been a beacon of light
You've lifted my spirits
Now I sleep well at night.

You make me smile
I can feel you care
You read my emails
Sometimes full of despair.

Yet you don't judge me
And that's what true friends do
So thankyou my friend
For just being you!.

Our Special Little Gift

I recall the doctor confirming, I am a "mother-to-be"
Mixed emotions I was feeling, of life growing in me!
My tummy swelled big, as over the months you grew,
Time was drawing near, soon I would be holding you.

You were born pink and screaming, sweetest sound I'd ever heard,
It would be 12 months later, when you said your first word.
Before long you were walking, getting up to no good,
You had Daddy wrapped around your finger, as I knew you would.

What did we do before you came along? Our lives were dull.
Now I'm picking up after you, cleaning finger prints off the wall.
You're our special little gift, we love you so much,
You've made us a family, you have a magic touch.

I should have seen it coming, we were playing on the front lawn,
Too close to the road, "Watch for cars!" I did warn,
The car was coming up the road, your Daddy he gave chase,
You thought he was playing, you thought it was a race.

The driver didn't see you, out in front you ran,
The screech of tyres I heard next, but what happened then?
Daddy held you in his arms, I was frozen to the spot,
You were limp and silent, my stomach in a knot.

The ambulance arrived from nowhere, they told us it looked grim,
They rushed you to hospital, this race you wouldn't win.
You held on for a little while, a battle you must have fought,
Although you were slipping fast, we couldn't stand the thought.

Your coffin was so tiny, it seemed so unfair,
Never again will we see you, or even stroke your hair.
Your Daddy and I miss you, we talk to you each day,
And every night before bed, a little prayer we say.

"Lord, keep our baby safe, don't let him be afraid,
And please don't punish him, for the mistake that we made.
Please give him cuddles, and kisses in the night,
Tell him he's home now, and everything's alright"

It's been a year since your passing, I put teddies on your grave,
I don't feel any stronger, I'm just not that brave.
I don't blame Daddy for leaving, I haven't been the best,
He's gone to start a new life; he says I need some rest.

You can't comprehend the pain, of what I feel inside,
I'm so desperate to see you, my feelings I can't hide.
I love you little Angel, so forgive me what I do,
I'll swallow this bottle of pills, just to be with you.

At last I see you there, my yearning hasn't been in vain,
Just as I always remember, your face it hasn't changed.
My beautiful little baby, I take your hand in mine,
Now we'll always be together, until the rest of time.

Man's Best Friend

My eyes are red and puffy, my face wet from crying,
"What's wrong?" people ask me. "It's my dog! My dog is dying!"
The insincerity it shows on their faces, they hide behind their lies,
"Oh? I'm sorry to hear that" they said, as they avert their eyes.

You've been my friend for years, but you never spoke a word
We communicated in our own way, through voices never heard.
I waited for that dreadful call, I knew it would come,
They had tried everything; this was your final run.

I stood looking down over you, as you lay there dying,
I wanted to be strong for you, instead of hopelessly crying.
Your big brown eyes looked at me, you knew your time had come,
There was no cure, it was over, The Reaper, he had won.

If we could only see, what is so obvious in the past,
Could I have done something, to make your time here last?
Life is surely a strange test, as it pulls your heart to bits,
If it's to build strength and character, then why is it just the pits?

I held your head gently, I cradled you against my chest,
I whispered, "I love you girl, go now in Heaven you'll rest".
I held you softly, stroking your face until you passed away,
My mind was numb with sadness, my best friend died today.

A gentle tap on my wrist, told me it was time to let you go.
But where would they take you? I really needed to know.
"Please don't put her on the floor! Her arthritis, it plays up!"
I still couldn't just let you go, I've had you from a pup.

Our home is so empty now, the backyard seems so big
It's so hard not seeing you here, or watching where you dig.
Then I heard a familiar sound, at the back door,
"Yes girl! I'm coming!" as I hear you bang your paw.

I realise then, I'm losing it, my mind is playing tricks
You're never coming home again, It's the Devil getting his kicks.
What I wouldn't give now, to see you chase your ball,
To play games and have some fun, as your name I would call.

I guess no point dwelling, on what I should have done,
Life just continues, just as the rising of the sun.
Memory of you won't fade, in the future near or far,
For a piece of me is missing, It's YOU! Where ever you are!

Holiday Adventure

Nana liked planes, holidays she would only fly,
That all changed, when she met this real strange guy.
Pa's thoughts of holidays, was only via sea,
Guess what Nana found out? A sailor he used to be.

They went on a cruise, a short one as a test,
When they came back Nana said, "it was the best".
"We got drunk and danced all night, Pa had to carry me back!"
I bet he was thrilled, as the weight she did stack.

Booze heads! The pair of you, a sight to behold,
Will you still be doing this, when you're really old?
New experiences Nana did learn, and please watch your head,
As you climbed in and out of, that little bunk bed.

Stuck at dinner tables, with people their own age,
"This is boring!" Nana says, "We want to RAGE!".
"Get the hip flask, Pa!" Nana cries, "I'm in need of a drink"
"Far out, Nana!" Pa replies, "Are you the missing link?".

They did manage to see some sights, but these tight wads wouldn't pay,
They checked out the cruise tours, then did it cheaper their own way.
Pleased as punch they found a cab, to take them around,
I guess it felt funny to them, to be on solid ground.

Is that the reason why, they rushed back to the ship?
Or were they just thirsty, and needed another sip?
I'm sure they must've done other stuff, the photos tell their fun,
Every photo is the same mind you, as they've latched on to someone.

They get home and unpack, their friends they must ring,
"Come see our photo's! and a pillow you must bring!".
Not long after they come back, Nana's checking out tours,
"Pa, we need an excuse. A birthday? How about yours?"

I'm Not A Little Boy

You do things for me, that you don't think I can
But Mum please look, I've grown into a man.
Mum, I want you to know, I don't need you in my life
I don't need you to look after me, I have a loving wife.

No, she won't replace you, or do things only you can do
But she is my choice, and I want you to love her too.
You have been a big part of my life, that I can't deny,
You would bandage me up, and hold me when I would cry.

You and Dad didn't make it, I guess I was only three,
So you had to be both roles, of parenting for me.
You didn't choose that role, no one could predict
You combined both roles by being soft and strict.

I turned out ok, I owe it all to you,
So don't judge me harshly, for doing the things I do.
I'm not a little boy, I do well for myself,
Now I've got a lovely home, I've even built a shelf.

I say I don't need you, and that has made you blue,
But I would prefer to **want you**, wouldn't you want that too?
When next time you see me, please see me as a man,
You've grown old too don't forget, old enough to be a Gran.

Yes! I May Be Old

You push past me, in a hurry to be on your way
What happened to manners? "Excuse me" is all you had to say.
Yes I may be old and slow, but please keep in mind,
If I had been younger, I'd have smacked your little behind.

You yell and honk at me, as I cross the road,
Why don't you get out your car, and help me with my load?
A bit of courtesy doesn't hurt, the world would be a better place,
Why do you rush about so much? Life is a journey not a race.

I can tell you things about how it was once done,
Before TV and radio and how the war was won.
You don't want to listen, I'm just an old fart
I'm amazed I've lived this long, I have a dicky heart.

Be nice it doesn't take much and please let get it right
How would you like to be me and pee 5 times a night?
I have no teeth left in my head, I had them all removed
A piece of steak I'd love to chew, but I can only gum my food.

If I sit and ramble on, and say the same thing twice
Don't roll your eyes at me, having visitors is nice.
I have to enjoy my own company, day in and day out
I'd love to go somewhere, but it's hard to get about.

Next time you go shopping, look at what's on the shelf
They're the foods I miss most, I can't reach them by myself.
The trolleys are so heavy, the wheels go everywhere
I struggle to get it going, while you just stand and stare.

And please don't get impatient, when at the checkout I do fumble
I can't hear what they say, these young ones they all mumble.
And how the hell do you expect me, to carry these plastic bags?
Back in my day however, we wrapped our food in rags.

We didn't know about recycling, or the ozone what was that?
So forgive me if I look at you, and think you're just a pratt.
We worked long hard hours, weekends weren't for rest
And we only had one set of clothes, we'd call our Sunday best.

A family was a solid unit, we all stayed together
Even when you got married, you came and lived with Mother.
Not these days apparently, you all do your own thing
So be it but when in trouble, family you do ring.

If I look weak and old when you visit, don't be afraid
And don't get too excited for no money did I save.
So pardon me if I bow out of your New Years Eve bash
I'm just an old fuddy duddy, who doesn't waste cash.

Tell Both Sides

I try so hard to say nothing and so I bite my tongue
But I can't help it now I've heard the story you tell everyone.
Please remember when you relate the tales about their Dad
Tell them the whole story, both sides are just as bad.

You didn't have much early on, their Dad worked a 7 day week
He couldn't see you needed more, you had reached your peak
You weren't there that night, frightened kids ever so small
Their Dad was crying so hard, as one by one your friends he did call.

I guess they punished you from then on, for making their Dad hurt
They didn't know what would happen, they were all on red alert
He came and told me quietly he still loved his beautiful wife
And that I shouldn't be mad with you, you were all he had in life.

He was big enough to forgive you, we were a family again
Although I guess for you both, life was never the same.
I don't judge or blame you, everyone makes mistakes
We live and learn for ourselves, sometimes rules we break.

You are both dear to me, I love you both the same
And it hurts to hear bad things, it causes needless pain.
You don't have to air your washing, in public have some pride
We all have skeletons in our closet, let's keep them locked inside.

So next time you put their Dad down, take a look into the crowd
To make very sure I won't hear, for my voice it will be loud.
Just accept you're not together, the memories are what you keep
Hold your tongues for long enough, the benefits you will reap.

Your hearts will be lifted, no chains tying you down
You will find peace and happiness no more will you frown.
Life is incredibly short, sadly our memories the same
If you can't say anything nice then just don't say his name.

I have said the same to him, he knows where I come from
We have had words over you, now he says no wrong.
Life shouldn't be spiteful, silly games that we play
Let's start the New Year off, let's make it all ok.

For My Friend

Our friendship is precious, it certainly means a lot,
A chance meeting one day, a bond formed on the spot.
You listen to my woes, with a smile and a frown,
You've heard some of my life, it certainly gets me down.

But still you don't judge me, nor ridicule my ways,
And when we meet up, we can talk for days!
What if others read, what is only for your eyes?
I'm sure we would shock them, we'd have to say "it's lies!".

You'd like my life, and some days I'd like yours,
Although it's not always what it seems, behind closed doors.
It's nice to have a friend, in whom I can confide
Sometimes I'm so bitter, my feelings I can't hide.

Just a little thankyou poem, from my heart to you
For driving from a far, and doing what you do.
I appreciate it so much, words just can't explain
You help ease my heartache, my sorrow and my pain.

I wish you joy, in everything that you do,
And please rely on me, to do the same for you!
This poem is for you my friend, I have to end it here,
May our friendship continue, throughout each and every year.

What You Mean To Me

Adopted out at birth, my life had only just begun
My parents hopes, were for a precious 2nd son.
Still I guess I was loved, was cared for and clean
It seems I've spent my whole life, living in a dream.

I wished I meant something, to my real Mum and Dad
For them I guess having a daughter, was pretty bad.
I craved for their approval, in everything I've done
I've always felt second best, for not being a son.

I've lived my life thinking, no one wants me around
I was always so lonely, had my chin on the ground.
I accepted second best in everything, jobs, love and marriage,
Then you came along, like a Prince leading a carriage.

You literally turned my crazy world upside down
You told me I'm not to cry and not to ever frown.
You took my friendship, and stored it deep in your heart,
"And there it will stay, 'til death do us part".

You told me you loved me, but I've been hurt before
This time is different, this time I'm really sure.
You're kind and loyal, you're not 2nd best,
What do you see in me? I'm not better than the rest.

You've placed your hands, gently in my heart
You've given me strength; I now see life has a start
So trusting and reassuring, I've never had before
Such love flowing around me, please let there be more.

Through my whole life I felt, that I just didn't exist
I was nothing to no one, then you appeared and life was bliss.
You hold me in your spotlight, you give me your smile
You are everything I live for, you make it all worthwhile.

To Live On Is Our Destiny

When I look in your eyes, I can see your pain
I know you still hold a candle, with an eternal flame.
If I could only be to you, what she obviously meant
I could ease your pain and give you love that's heaven sent.

It's no sin for a man to cry, so just let your tears flow
You'll find some new love, but just when we do not know.
Each of us is here for a reason, it's not for us to question God why,
We have to trust in Him, and accept his decisions who die.

You don't need to stop living, her memory will always live on
I don't want to erase that, I just hope you'll be strong.
You'll meet her again one day, but please let's not rush
Life is very brief and Father Time does not hush.

He ticks on and on and steals our seconds away,
Don't you realise, we have less and less every day?
I loved her too don't forget, she meant everything to me
But we're still here, to live on is our destiny.

For a man to lose his wife, it seems so unkind
Just look around and you will see what's left behind.
My arms are open, my heart is breaking for you,
Please hold me Daddy, for I'm grieving too.

Meant To Meet

I'm glad I've come to know you, everything has a reason
I bet we were meant to meet, in that summer season.
Working side by side in the office and taking angry calls
At times working in Sydney, had us climbing up the walls.

Time went on, friendships sprout, as they usually do
You make it very comfortable, to pour out my heart to you.
It's probably not fair on you, for me to whine like a clown
You have you own qualms, I know they get you down.

You get so sad, if only there was something I could do
The best I have to offer, is just to sit and listen to you.
There's nothing I can say at this time, to make you feel better
I like to give you a giggle, so sometimes I write you a letter.

My life I make sound exciting, it's at best my imagination
But if you read between the lines, you'll hear my frustration.
I take what I have and colour it up, make it really bright
Without this special effect, it's pretty much all black and white.

If we swapped lives for a day, I'm sure you would find
It's not what I crack it up to be, you'd probably lose your mind.
It's not the job or the house or the dogs, that make you go on,
It's the inner self of pride, filling your heart with song.

It's knowing that you've won, the hurdles of the past
And accepting that the hard times, won't always last.
It's looking at what we have, and dreaming of what's to come
Or seeing the funny side, even if there really isn't one.

It's taking in a view, or a spectacular sun rise
Just smiling for no reason, or remembering little white lies.
It's about being independent and being proud to be you,
Being able to love ourselves and accepting what you do.

Just get it right in your mind, and the rest it will follow,
Life doesn't have to be a bitter pill that's too hard to swallow.
Remember tears are made of water, don't waste a precious drop
If you spill them on the floor, you'll have to get the mop!!

So what good is a day, in one you didn't smile?
Life is very brief, we're only here for a short while.
So do your best with what you have, mistakes are here to be made
I agree it's easier to just not bother, but why not be brave?

Congratulations – On Your Engagement

Fabulous news to hear, I'm so happy for you two,
Love is very precious, it's a wonderful thing to do.
Show the world you love her, and never be shy,
For she's made her commitment, you're the apple of her eye.

When the big day comes, and you take her as your bride,
Give all your world for her, she'll fill your heart with pride.
And when you accept this role, to be his loving wife,
Take the oath seriously, and love him all your life.

Don't say hurtful things to each other, They are so hard to undo,
They can make the deepest wounds, and break a heart in two.
Just accept that you have differences, And love each other for that,
That's what you liked in the beginning, Opposites do attract.

To two very happy people, Enjoy your life together,
Remember to be great lovers, And a friend to each other.
Enough of my lecture, I'm sure these words aren't new,
I wish you both all the very best, And CONGRATULATIONS to you!

Daddy Gave His Little Girl Away

My life with you, is more words than I can write,
I remember the times, I used to sneak home at night.
You would be ready for golf, In the early morning,
And startle me completely, I had to stifle my yawning.

We didn't have many moments, that affected just you and I,
But my wedding day was one, I hoped we wouldn't cry.
I was so proud of you that day, you looked like a King,
I was your little Princess, but we couldn't say anything.

On the way to the Church, you held both my hands tight,
I didn't mind it at all, it felt incredibly right.
Very comforting and assuring, I was going to be a wife,
I was glad I had my Dad with me, I needed him in my life.

I couldn't tell you then, what I can tell you now,
But I'd do it all again with you, give me away to say a vow.
It was wonderful to be with you, On my big day out,
It was wonderful to sit and hold you, without having to shout.

You walked me down that Church aisle, All poised and calm,
And on the Priests command, you passed over my arm.
Daddy gave his little girl away; would she forget him now?
Would she still need him, even after she's said her vow?

Of course, I'll still need you, because "I love you this much!"
You are my first love, No one can or will "replace" you as such.
This wonderful beautiful memory I have, Of just you and I,
Will stay with me always, even as time goes by.

First Love

Standing out in the sun, amongst a whole lot
You laid eyes on me, you said I looked "hot".
You ran your hands over my body, your eyes grew wide,
I couldn't wait to show you, what I had inside.

You said I was the best, better than any other
You couldn't wait to take me home, show me to your mother
Your mates were pretty envious, they all patted you on the back
When you refused to share me, they thought you were slack.

We had many hours together, the moments we had were great.
I didn't mind waiting for you, at the club you were always late.
I know you looked at others, I had no reason to fear
I know you touched & fondled the others, especially their rear,

There are lots to admire, gorgeous model types
They all had bits you liked, but you said I was just right.
You made me squeal, you knew how to handle me
You drove me hard and fast, we are a pleasure to see.

As with all first loves, your lust wore off.
As I got older, I developed a bad cough.
You soon tired of the attention, I was demanding
You started to complain, your bank account I was draining.

One day you traded me in, for a much sharper look,
She was a real beauty, I know you got caught in her hook
You'll never forget me, no matter where you are,
Because no man ever forgets about, his very first car.

Work Friends

I first met you in October, it was the year 1998,
Starting in sales, you didn't know your fate.
We were both quiet and shy, but I offered you advice,
Keep to yourself don't get involved, and people will be nice.

The owners came in one day, and I told you what I think,
"You know?" I said, "they are pushing me to the brink!".
Sadly I did not heed, my own piece of valuable wisdom,
And before long things fell apart for me, at the Corporate Kingdom.

I upset the apple cart, oh at least a million times,
And I lost count of the days I told you, "I've just resigned!".
But you would be there for me, with blocks of chocolate in tow,
"This'll cheer you up!" you'd say, "Not much longer to go".

I don't know why we got excited, when 4.30pm rolled around,
We would still be there working, when the 6pm bell would sound.
Was it dedication or devotion, that we sacrificed our time?
Or are we just bloody stupid? Work should be a crime.

We had our laughs though, usually at someone else's expense,
Remember when we sucked in helium, Under the marquee tents?
Remember the Christmas party? Staff functions I do dread.
You had a Christmas tree, growing right out of your head!

You earned a promotion, and I wished you the best of luck,
Is this the worse job you've ever had, just to earn a buck?
You do it really well, but your stress it sometimes shows,
Now you've got them all doing ballet, Dancing on their toes!!

I just had silly rhymes, going through my head,
I had to put these to paper, before I went to bed.
So Lovely girl just be happy, with what you want to do,
And remember to please only one person, and that person is YOU!

I'm Not Married To You

I watch you through the window, your eyes and face so set,
What would you say if I told you, I wished we never met?
Would you say you felt the same, it's a mistake our lives entwine?
Would you say you were blameless, and the fault it was all mine?

I feel torn when I see you, but I wished it wasn't true
The fact is I belong to someone, but that someone isn't you.
We torture ourselves with hope, as we carefully plan our day,
I eagerly wait for you, as I watch him drive away.

We steal minutes at a time, we both know it's a deadly game,
Hoping no one will get hurt, our lives won't ever be the same.
Why then do I crave to meet you? Why then must I tell lies?
Why then don't I care, if he reads deception in my eyes?

I want it all to be over, I want my life to return,
I just want one of you, what lesson did I learn?
I learnt how easy it is to fall, by kind words and affection,
I learnt loving isn't easy, when you go in a different direction.

I learnt loving isn't simple, I have it confused with lust,
So how do you clearly distinguish, which one is a "must"?
I picture what is happening, and how I feel today,
And then how would I react, if the roles were around the other way?

Would I be so mad with him, that I would cause him harm?
Or would I simply want to ask him, to hold me in his arms?
Would I understand the reason, for him wanting someone new?
Or would I be so devastated, I wouldn't know what to do?

Well that will never happen, because I trust him so,
I don't deserve the likes of him, so he must never know.
He must never find out, what actions I have done,
For I am now so wracked with guilt, the excitement it's all gone.

You must leave me now, for I am so full of sorrow,
You must never come back here, don't even think about tomorrow.
It will be very hard for me, my feelings are deep and true,
For I am in love with you both, but I am not married to you.

Don't Forget This Friend

I've known you a long time,
Well at least, thirty years
Our hearts have been broken,
Our eyes filled with tears.

We've journeyed through a lifetime
And sometimes slammed the door
But I want you to know
Mine's open for you just once more

You're welcome in my world
But I'm not sure I'm welcome in yours
True friends seem hard to find
I don't think you are a lost cause.

I too have known pain and loss
No need to suffer it all on your own
Just keep in touch once in a while
You'll see my friendship is not a loan.

My friendship is a gift for you
I wish you could see that
I hope each day you'll use it
It's the same as a welcome mat.

So don't forget this friend
Who doesn't judge and isn't shocked
The one who's hoping you'll come by
The one who's door is never locked.

Children Need Love

On occasions like these, I like to write.
Life's little mysteries, inspire me at night.
What happened to my youth? Pigtails and giggles.
I still think I could dance to the Wiggles.

All those years gone, in a blink of an eye.
What is life about then? I have to ask why.
As a child you have to obey, conform and trust.
Mistakes aren't allowed, but mistakes are a must.

How many parents say, "We know what's best for you".
Let them find out for themselves, as it's their life too.
We're not exact replica's, each different in our own way.
Some are sportsmen or scholars, while some just want to play.

If everything seemed easy, we'd still complain.
We'd say we were bored, life's always the same.
But every now and then, we take a bumpy route.
While some pull through, others go down the chute.

But it's wonderful to know, you dealt with it your way.
The mistake you made last time, aren't the same you make today.
We live in a world that's fast paced and hurried.
There is no time to relax, everyone looks so worried.

But if you looked at your life, up high from miles in space.
The silence is deafening, and you can't see the rat race.
Games you played as a child, are no longer fun for you.
You must grow up, behave, like responsible adults do.

Children laugh so often, we think their cartoons are dumb.
And heaven forbid, if for comfort adults sucked their thumb.
Children have no pressures, curiosity make them learn.
Adults want all the answers now, adults can't wait their turn.

Children just want love, they simply trust everyone.
As adults we know, that strangers carry a gun.
Children have imagination, a fantasy world is real.
Adults crush that, as we 'fess up to the "Santa" spiel.

Children believe in the Easter Bunny, he brings chocolate eggs.
Adults complain about the cost, and grumble over it in bed.
Children don't care about, colour, religion or race.
Adults change that, we make them see they're out of place.

So if children are, the world's absolute delight.
Why do adults tell stories, and make them fear the night?
Children are our precious gifts, we treat them indifferently
But just remember, they will out live the likes, of you and me.

If so much trouble and unrest globally, causes us worry.
Why do we make our children, grow up in such a hurry?
The world attitude could change, in the space of a generation.
Let's adopt the innocence of children, and have a friendlier nation.

So all the while we blame this, on our parents and theirs.
We only make it worse, and give ourselves grey hairs.
Children don't care, that Barbie dolls are plastic.
Women's lib has gone crazy, it's really quite drastic.

What's right and what's wrong, with childhood.
Is ruined by the minority, and doesn't do any good.
Let the children play, let them enjoy life.
Don't cast them aside, when you run into strife.

We do so much harm, as we "protect our little ones".
It's only our point of view, but I'm sure they have some.
So listen to your children, as they make up a story.
Fighting of dragons, and accolades of glory.

Children just want to please, don't deny them the pleasure.
You may regret later on, those moments you didn't treasure.
Adults blame their misdemeanours, on their childhood years.
Why is it not embarrassing to say, your parents caused your tears?

If 10 years from now, your "baby" gets into strife.
Could you say honestly, "I gave them love all their life".
Could you say truthfully, "They had my undevoted time".
Or are you partly responsible, for their life of crime?

Are you too tired after work, to hear what they say?
They just want to share with you, what happened in their day.
Are you too busy cleaning house, to see what they've made?
Mess will be there tomorrow, but your children have changed.

If you push them aside, they'll believe they mean nothing.
They'll always be missing, that special "something".
No one else can give them, that strong parental bond.
Early years are so crucial, you can't wave a magic wand.

Are you a person searching, for your parents attention?
Never having it as a child, you didn't learn affection?
Still craving and yearning, for your parents to see
You realise, you didn't turn out what they wanted you to be?

So you're not rich, or a beautiful movie star.
But you are what you are, and you've made it this far.
Did you sit in your bedroom as a child, night after night?
Did you become withdrawn, did you hear all their fights?

I am soon to give birth, my God what have I done?
I hope I'm not disappointed, if it's not born a son.
I hope I don't fall, into your parents mould.
And not hear my kids cry, wanting their mum to hold.

I hope I don't punish them, for coming along.
It's I who conceived them, they did no wrong.
I hope I'll always love them, they're my flesh and blood.
And enjoy watching them bloom, like a tiny new bud.

I hope I don't get weary, and want something new.
"I'm tired of these kids now, what else can I do?"
I hope I don't stop loving them, because their dad left town.
Never let me say bad things about him, when they are around.

I hope they know how much I love them, by little things I do.
And before I lose my temper, remember to count past two.
I hope I give them the childhood, full of wonderful memories.
Lots of days spent laughing, and climbing up trees.

I hope I give them encouragement, to always tell the truth.
Even the elaborate stories, of disenchanted youth.
I hope that when my time is over, and I depart this earth.
They will be happy to know, I loved them for all it's worth.

Why let the ways of the past, ruin the best to come?
You can't change the yesterdays, you know what must be done.
I have my own life now, being an adult sometimes is hard
Don't look back in anger, just because you're scarred.

When You're Away

You've gone away, and left me alone.
You know how I get, here on my own.
Bored and restless, at the same time,
There's plenty to do, but nothing springs to mind.

Getting the fire started, is my number one job,
I still burn my fingers, I yell but won't sob.
Then I get mesmerised, and the flames I just stare,
And I imagine you're sitting here in your chair.

There's ironing to do, yeah some other time,
I could do some washing, but I have no spare line.
I could always cook something, for one it's a pain,
Or I could sit here, whinge, write and complain?

I could imagine you're here, snuggled up with me,
That's just too hard, so I'll just make some tea.
Even the dogs are feeling, quite strange of late,
They wander around, lost and looking for their mate.

I hope you are happy, and finding your way,
It's important to know, you get something from each day.
I know you love planes, you're such a big kid,
Make the most of it, and be glad you did.

Not long now, and you'll be home here soon,
Only one more sleep and it's a full moon.
Sadly Monday will come, and you'll leave again,
My heart will then break, and be filled with pain.

But absence makes the heart grow fonder,
And before long, my mind it will wander.
I'll daydream about, what we can do,
And as always, never ever stop loving you.

Where Did We Go Wrong?

What happened to us? It's not the same anymore.
I just want to poke your eyes out, and slam you head into a door.
You take me for granted, I get so mad at you.
There are days when I wish, you and I were through.

Have we tired of each other? Was our love short lived?
Is there nothing left between us? Is there nothing left to give?
Has the excitement of our new home, dawned into realisation
That we have little money spare, and is the cause of our frustration?

I've changed my entire life for you, and I feel nothing in return.
I'm afraid you're bored with me, It's just your love that I yearn.
Please stop the tension, that's building between you and I.
Let's make a deal right now, to laugh rather than cry.

If this is all I ask, can you do your best?
Will you love me tenderly, or will you fail my test?
Will you take this seriously, or do you say the fault is all mine?
We have to listen to each others needs, if we are to make it this time.

Rascal – My Loyal Dog

You came into our lives, A stray dog with no home,
I took you in and fed you, no more did you roam.
13 years ago that happened, you gave us love and loyalty,
It's now my turn to repay, and give you some final dignity.

I've braced myself for this day, when no longer you'll be here,
But I'll have to tell you Rascal, I've shed nothing but tears.
You have suffered in your final days, that will always be my regret,
I said my goodbyes to you today, on the last trip to your vet.

Your pain will haunt me always, but I held you while you died,
It still hasn't sunk in, even though I've cried and cried.
At last your suffering is over, you did look like you were asleep,
I hugged you and kissed you, you made not a sound, not a peep.

Please forgive me Rascal, for ending your life,
The sadness I am feeling, it cuts like a knife.
Time heals all wounds, and do you believe in fate?
The little dog I brought home 2 days ago, is now Vee's new mate.

Decisions made all through life, sometimes leave regret,
And I'm so sorry we decided it would be your final trip to the Vet.
If this was a perfect world, you'd be the perfect friend,
You'd never have to die, and your time would never end.

I just can't believe Rascal, that you've really gone.
I hope you know it wasn't because, you had done anything wrong.
Thankyou Rascal, for being my best friend,
For being so loving and loyal, until your very end.

Rascal – I Miss You

My sweet Rascal, I miss you so very much.
All I have is memories, but it's you I'd rather touch.
You rocked my world on your passing, I've tried so hard to be strong.
But the tears they just keep flowing, all day and all night long.

I look at your photo's, they do make me smile.
From little puppy to adulthood, you were a rogue there for a while.
My heart isn't just broken, it's shattered into bits,
Putting the pieces back together, the pain is just the pits.

I have to "soldier on" they say, my life mustn't end here,
I still have my other dog, who I also love very dear.
He is not the same anymore, I'm sure he misses you,
So between the pair of us, our world is very blue.

He won't sleep in the kennel now, that you and he once shared,
I'm not sure what he'll do, and in my heart I'm scared.
Oh Rascal if you can hear me, can you come back home?
I want you back so much, I don't want you to be alone.

My tears are now flowing, from up in heaven can you see?
Please come back for Christmas, I need you back with me.
Rascal I'll never forget you, to me you meant so much,
There'll never be another you, for my heart you have touched.

Daughters Can Be Friends

Why do you make me feel, I've always done something wrong?
The only crime I committed was not being born your son.
And spiteful words, can cause hurt so deep,
Do you know the meaning, of "you sow what you reap"?

I can't imagine, what a disappointment I've been,
And is it you I should blame, for my low self-esteem?
Do you think you'll ever want to be my friend?
Or is it like looking for a rainbow, that never ends?

Is it too hard, or will it take up too much time?
We will never know, if we give up trying.
So many times, we've come down this road,
Why then does it seem, I carry the entire load?

I am trying to focus, on something good and positive,
It's very draining, seeing the world always negative.
I think you need also, to try something new,
I think you need help, but what else can I do?

I guess that's really, the whole nuts and bolts,
We don't accept each other, with our imperfect faults.
I'm sad for you, I didn't turn out to be a son,
But I am your daughter; I am your only one.

Maybe one day, you'll wake up and see,
I'm not the witch; you make me out to be.
I hope that day, doesn't come too late,
Just pray it's well before, you're at the Pearly Gates.

What a waste then, it would be,
If you realise the true friend, you could've had in me.
Until that day, I just pray and wish,
For the love of my family, that I sadly miss.

Confusion

Why is it when you're gone,
My thoughts and feelings are so strong?
I blow you a kiss and wave you goodbye
But really, I just want to cry.

I wear a brave face I put it on for show
I guess it's because I don't want people to know.
A sad song or I think I hear your voice
Reduces me to tears like I have no choice.

So then why do I keep you at full arm's length?
Why not embrace you and defy my act of strength?
Why not tell you I love you and mean it when I say?
Why do I always feel I should push you away?

I know the answers to my questions of fear
I know the truth; I know it's all up here.
I'm afraid to get close, afraid of what could happen
I tell myself I can manage if it all ended quite sudden.

But why am I wasting time wondering about the "what if's?"
I should be enjoying my time with you, reality is stiff.
I think I've wished for love for so long now
I'm a little bit scared it will fade with a vow.

You truly are the guiding angel I prayed I would find
You make me think and feel different you are one of a kind.
If I look into my heart I wonder what surprises are there
I bet fate played a hand and gave me a soul mate, to love and care.

Vee – My Precious Dog

I've had you furever, you were merely 6 weeks old,
I promised I would look after you, a promise I must uphold.
I will NOT let you suffer, nor will I leave you in pain,
So I find myself making, the hardest decision again.

I've watched you stumble, watched as your legs did fail
I've listened as your breathing got rattly, you were growing frail.
Your hearing is no longer, and your teeth are weak and few,
I ask myself why does this have to happen, to a special puppy like you?

Your big brown eyes, so responsive and alert
Your mind knew what it wanted, but your body wouldn't work.
Your lumps now protruding, like tennis balls in you,
I'm so sorry, there's very little left that we can actually do.

You're nearly 14 now, my brown furry friend,
I know you don't think so, but it's close to your end.
Like a young man trapped in an old mans body,
Your eyes pleaded and begged, and yes I'm so very sorry.

You were my hero, as you resigned to your fate,
We all sat on the floor, for the Vet we did wait.
I laid on you and cradled you in my arms tight,
I wanted you to not feel alone, when they turned out your light.

Well my little buddy, I kissed you my final goodbye,
And I am not ashamed, of all the tears that I have cried.
If only I worked miracles, instead of playing God,
No pet would ever die, and you'd still be my faithful dog.

You're now set free, from your cancer and arthritic pain,
Fly your soul upwards, and be with Rascal again.
So now my 2 precious friends, will have each other just once more,
And probably cause as much havoc up there, as you did here before.

Relationship Blues

We met whilst on holidays, in fact upon a ship
I was attracted to you, a secret on my lips.
Back in the cabin, our bodies did entwine
The memory is exquisite; I'd even say divine.

Early days of "courting", the excitement in our eyes
I'm happy to say the excitement, has never died.
I know you feel the same; the magic is still there
So let's stop all the hurt, if we really care.

Why do we argue, fight and call names?
Two adults reverting, back to childish games.
We suffer so much, and harbour great pain
We break up and make up and do it all again.

You are my world, and yet you just can't see
That it's only with you, I just want to be
My heart I proudly wear, in full view on my sleeve
So bound up with love, like a web you did weave.

How did this start? And where will it go?
This relationship of ours, I just need to know.
I love you so much, I swear on the spot I'd die
If you said it's not worth it, that you didn't want to try.

So many years of caring, loving and sharing with you
I can't walk away from this now; it's not in me to do
I want so much for us; I'm in this for life
As I dare to dream of us, becoming man and wife.

You know we can make it; we're batting on the same side
We both want much the same, so why the bumpy ride?
There's no one else for me, and the same is said for you
So let's get our act together, and work at what to do.

Life can be over in an instant, so are the arguments legit?
Don't you think the pair of us, exaggerate a tiny bit?
We still have so much love, we are abusing God's gift
He created man and woman to be together, not to cause a rift.

Think of those who perished, at ages oh so incredibly young
In Bali they were bombed, never again to see their loved one.
Put it into perspective, we have a choice in life
Or we can ask those left behind, how much they miss their wife.

We could ask those agonizing, from sorrow and despair
And let them hear our problems, and ask if they would care.
We should live each day, as if this were our last
For I really think there's a lesson here, we should grasp.

If today was my final day, to live and breathe on Earth
I would spend it with you, and enjoy it for what it's worth.
I guess that's the whole story, in its simplest form
And that I'd always pick you, to hug and keep me warm.

Moe – My Cheeky Little Kitten

You were my fluffy ball of a kitten
First baby I have held in a long time
You had beautiful piercing blue eyes
You were so adorable I had to make you mine.

Your personality so strong and confident
You made me smile to watch you play
You would get into mischief and strife
And you always got things going your way.

On my bed you would sleep
Curled up in my arms tight
You just loved being cuddled
You simply purred all night.

You were just my little ball of trouble
You felt the world was yours to own
You tempted fate once too often
Now I will never see you fully grown.

You have left me magic memories
I feel so lucky to have had you
And I am sad that you didn't grow old
But I think that's something you already knew.

You were so full of life and adventure
I think you were a message from above
The message is to not take anything for granted
And give all of yourself when you give love.

Well my precious little Moe
It's time for me to say goodbye
I know the Angels are looking after you
I hope you never make them cry.

English Rose

Don't be sad, that I have gone
Don't dwell too much, about my death so young.
I have much to tell you, much to confess,
And if you believe in miracles, you'll understand this mess.

A Mothers love, is so deep and is so strong,
That we mothers hope and pray, nothing will go wrong.
We fuss and we fret, with childhood diseases,
We nurse you through coughs, colds, flu's and the sneezes.

When you got really sick, and things looked grim,
I'd close my eyes and say an anxious prayer to Him.
"Please Lord, give this sickness to me,
And just let my children be healthy and free".

The good Lord always listened, and always came through,
And he would say "In time I need Angels like you",
Well the date he did set, for the Lord He needed me,
And He gave me fair warning, so with you all I could be.

He sent His Angels down, to see me the night before,
They spoke to me and told me, about this life and more,
If only I could ease your pain, and tell you what lies before you,
I know you wouldn't be sad, and you will all pull through.

We united as a family and braved it all through till the end,
I am saddened you are all grieving, if only rules I could bend.
But promises made with the Lord, are not to be broken,
My time here is up; the last word has been spoken.

To my 3 precious children, that I breathed life into,
You filled my heart with pride and I will always love you,
To my darling Husband, of so many years,
Take care of our children, and allay all their fears.

I say farewell now to my family and friends,
But please don't think this is the end,
There's another place far more rewarding and true,
And in this place, I will be waiting to see all of you

In loving memory of Mary

What Do You Do?

What do you do, when the love fades away?
When years of marriage, can't make you stay.
When looking in his eyes for a hint of care,
And all that looks back is a cold cold stare?

What do you do, when he dismisses your needs?
When you scream inside for caresses and dreams?
What do you feel when a relationship goes bad?
Sheer and utter emptiness, nothing is more sad.

What do you do, when questions you ask,
Aren't answered, but you're taken to task?
What do you feel, when emotionally you're drained?
When you see all the problems, and feel you're the blame?

Just _what_ do you do, this is where I'm at,
What _should_ I feel, I can't answer that.
When do you know, it's time to move on?
I wish _I_ knew, because I can't answer that one.

Sad Memories Welcome You

Why do you cry at night all alone?
Why do you break down and sob, when you get home?
What place do you go to, when your mind takes you for walks?
And what does it say, when you listen to it talk?

Why is this place, so cold and so bleak?
And why is it <u>this</u> place, for comfort you seek?
What world <u>is</u> it, that draws you there?
Why can't you see, it's full of despair?

Why do you harbour, your pain so deep?
And only in <u>this</u> world, it robs you of sleep?
Why do you settle here, for hours on end?
Sad memories welcome you, like a very old friend.

Why are you content, to let songs drag you down?
Why can't you put the brakes on, before you hit the ground?
Regrets and memories of the past, you allow to consume you
Why grieve over them, there's nothing more you can do?

Please stop the roller coaster, of this emotional distress
I beg you to watch the signs, which lead to this mess.
Please say goodbye, to the demons and more,
Please close this chapter, and don't re open the door.

Whatever turned you, into this chaotic wife,
Can be cut from you, with a spiritual knife.
Don't let the sadness, destroy the good times ahead
So STOP writing sad poems, and get back to bed!

My Resume

Here is my introduction, quite different from the rest
I'm sure you will remember it, amongst the very best.
Let me know, if I stand out from the crowd.
As a potential employee, I could make you very proud.

Decisions to be made, and deadlines to meet,
No time wasting for me, I think on my feet.
I am not racist, discriminatory, nor am I naïve,
And rarely in my work history, have I had sick leave.

My work ethics, Are second to none.
I believe in doing it right, to get the job done.
Doting your I's, And crossing your T's
This is second nature to me; I find doing it a breeze.

I love a challenge; It's a mental test.
So, when I take it on, I give it my best.
I am sensitive to others; I enjoy a laugh and joke.
But time is money, and no I don't smoke.

Numbers are my passion; my records are clean.
But I can adapt to change, without causing a scene.
If this is what you're looking for, then please give me a call.
You won't be disappointed you did, in no way at all.

Vale - Grandma

I knew you as Grandma; I had enormous respect for you
You welcomed me into your fold, as a most natural thing to do.
I enjoyed our lengthy chats; I know we should have had more
And that's when reality bites and emotions become raw.

We said our goodbyes to you, in a beautiful send off today
So many friends and family, all with lovely things to say.
I wasn't surprised by the numbers and everything they said is true
You touched so many lives, by simply being you.

It doesn't seem real, tell me they got it all wrong
Because I can't quite picture what will happen now that you've gone.
Who will keep the family a circle, if you I can no longer ring?
Who will prick our conscience about doing the right thing?

I hope you knew I loved you, maybe I only told you twice
Actions speak louder than words, the cross stitch was my vice.
You were a witness at our wedding, a true Matriarch
We never considered any other and it meant so much to Mark.

You will not be forgotten, we planted a rose bush in your memory
It is the best looked after Rose, from Heaven you'll see.
It's true you are already enormously missed, our lives a little numb
Not only were you a terrific Grandma, but also a wonderful Mum.

Nan

I love you so much Nan, I miss what we once had
I'm gutted you don't remember, Dementia is so sad.
But only for those around you, watching you go downhill
As the disease takes more of your mind, seemingly at will.

I am weak as I make lots of excuses, my visits are too few
I find it impossible to accept, there's nothing anyone can do.
You confuse me with others; this stabs me in the heart
I am angry with God and ask why did he let this disease start.

I should just accept it, and be blessed it's not hurting you
You would take no pleasure in knowing; it makes us all so blue.
So I'd like you to know now, before you forget this day
That I love you Nan and I wish it wasn't ending this way.

I know one thing for sure, when you eventually get called home
You'll be swearing at the Angels, and demanding to be shown.
Just where in this book of life it says, you can waste your years
And die whilst still living and cause unnecessary tears.

If there's a lesson to learn, throughout this whole ordeal
That's don't take tomorrow for granted, life can be surreal.
Tell people you love them now, before they're gone too soon
Then you won't carry the guilt around, like an open wound.

My Naughty Little Boy

I lost my two dogs, in their veteran years
The pain still stabs me and brings me to tears.
So I wasn't certain, I could go through this again
"Ridgebacks for Sale", my curiosity did begin.

When I saw you and all your littermates
My eyes teared up, the emotions were raked.
I felt almost guilty, looking and cuddling you
I felt as though I was betraying, my loyal other two.

You looked nothing like them, and for that I am glad
I can't ever replace them; it would only make me sad.
You have a wonderful nature and are such a joy.
You are mischievous and boisterous, my naughty little boy.

I just smother you with kisses and you kiss me right back
Your tiny features so cute, you little bum I could smack.
How quick you are growing; I blink and you change
The garden is too tempting and our plants you rearrange.

You seem so fragile; you have me under your spell
I have babied you no end, now you give me hell.
You don't listen to instructions; you drive me up the wall
You continue to ignore me, when your name I call and call.

But just when I believe you won't learn, you surprise me no end
You know sit, drop and stay, as you want to be my friend.
Many years you will be with us, I look forward to each one
Although some days I do wonder, just what is to come?

"Ivy" Moments And Memories

Her name is Ivy but known as Mum, Ive, Granny Grunt and Nan
Many more names I shouldn't repeat, I don't think I can.
Married to Bert for 50 years, sadly he isn't with us any more
A true gentleman, hard to imagine he fought in the war.

Speaking of War, Bert was called up, Ivy joined voluntarily
She loved Bert; she joined up so with him she could be.
Bert was fighting in a foreign land, and got a fright of his life
Who did he see standing there? It was Ivy, his wife!!

"Hello Berty. I followed you here. What do you think of that?"
"I'd recognise you anywhere, even disguised in your slouch hat".
So three days they were given, to reacquaint wedded bliss
It was a few years later, when once again they would kiss.

Two children they had, a quiet daughter and a noisy son
One would ride motorbikes; the other wanted to be a Nun.
A photo I recollect, of Nan on the back of Phil's motorbike
How stunning she did look, as her dress she did hike.

All her dogs were "Rusty", I thought they were one and the same
She laughs every time I ask "why didn't you change their name?"
Cursing and swearing, cigarette hung out the side of her lips
She wasn't one to mess with, with hands on her hips.

Sex education care of Nan, as Grandkids our eyes wide
As she told dirty ditties especially "Rise penis, Rise!"
Who could forget the one "Little fly upon the wall"
And we all chimed in with,"Ain't you got no clothes at all?"

Our parents never knew, just how much we were being taught
Our Nan was extremely clever and she never got caught.
We knew how to swear and in what context too
And all the while our parents never had a clue.

Jade in her early teens wagged school and caught a cab
She'd arrive at Nan's, who would fix up the tab.
Nan knew Jade, should have been at school.
Nan never told her parents, our Nan was real cool.

I did her housework, I cleaned and vacuumed the hall,
I wondered how she managed to get muck this high up the wall.
She loved her independence, with neighbours she would fight
She'd watched them come and go and always thought she was right.

Helen took her out, so off in a wheelchair they did set
Helen pushed and pulled Nan around, and worked up a sweat.
Was there anything malicious in it, or was it just an accident
Nearly tipping Nan out of the wheelchair and on to the pavement.

If only Helen could stop laughing, whilst telling this tale
Nan was not as delighted, it took the wind out her sail.
No more trips in the chair with chrome wheels,
Not that Helen could really manage to push it up those hills.

She is the Matriarch of the family, with its ever-growing brood
Lucky she isn't able to teach the new generation, how to be rude.
Five Grandchildren, and Great Grandchildren now totalling six
Please don't look at me, to add to this mix.

There are many more moments and memories, all lost in time
To list them all it would be a long and never ending rhyme.
And even though she's unable to remember anything too clear
She is swearing and making me laugh, while she is still here.

Corporation Shame

Please don't ever think, that I believe you won
You used bullyboy tactics to beat your war drum.
Your bias and hostility was despicable to say the least
In effect all this did, was unleash the slumbering beast.

She fought for her reputation, you shredded it with slander
She dealt you 52 allegations; to you she would not pander.
You fought your arguments with your lawyers and your lies
She fought her arguments with only the truth and her pride.

You were all being played, by people higher up the chain
You should never forget that, as it will always be your shame.
You failed her with investigations of taping on her phone
You sent her hostile letters and told her to remain at home.

Not once did you seem to care to find out the whole truth
She felt as though she was shouting in the wind on top of a roof.
The double standards that you applied when playing this game
Has tainted and buried the good out of your Corporate name.

Life has not stopped for her, nor will she get stuck in this rut
Believe me it would take better than you, to crack this nut.
Enjoy your work choice career, I will certainly enjoy mine
Just next time you try this on, get all the facts the first time.

Vale – Ivy Grace – In Loving Memory Of My Nan

Born Ivy Grace, 6th January Nineteen Eighteen
Was a stunning young lady, Every man's dream.
But it was butcher boy Bert that finally caught her eye
And she fixed her sights on him because she certainly wasn't shy.

She did join the WAFS, to be with Bert as was her will
But he sent her straight back home and told her to chill.
They had two children and Ivy brought home more
She worked in a mother & babies home, well after the war.

So caring and courageous, she took in all the waifs and strays
Two and four legged, she helped them in many ways.
But it was defending her own brood, which made her blood boil
Her tongue-lashing and temper, made many a man recoil.

Certainly larger than life, in plenty of ways I can't explain
Her ditties, her drama's, her unique expressions remain.
They aren't easily forgotten, they make us all smile
They get stuck in your head and go around for a while.

Enjoy this now, on your next journey Ivy Grace
And when you get there, don't have "that" look on your face.
I bet you're already giving it to Bert, just the same
No doubt you'll be giving it to us too, when we meet again.

No sad farewell poems, no goodbyes to say
We all know what you meant to us, no need to replay.
Just take care of yourself and mind how you go,
And we'll catch up with you again before you know.

Wingless Angel

I watch you tend to others so devoted and caring
Concentration intent on your face
Then you look up and see me
And a warm feeling in my heart you place.

You surely are a Wingless Angel,
Sent from Heaven to spread your love
They broke the mould after they made you,
So precious and perfect like a little white dove.

You had your own hands full but never complain
You gave so unselfishly and fussed over my Nan
Not only her, you looked out for everyone
Nothing was too much while you cared for your man.

Your compassion for strangers, is undeniably pure
It was fate that our paths crossed again in this life
You make me wish you were my mother
And no doubt you have always been an awesome wife.

Sadly now our paths in life have come to a fork
Thankyou is not enough, but it's a great start
Because of you my Wingless Angel
You've left footprints in my heart.

The Years That Separate Us

The years have passed and the book was closed
Then like a gift from the Gods, you suddenly arose.
When you held me in your arms so tight,
It was a vivid memory of when things were right.

Somehow I feel in those arms I belong
And yet somehow I know It's just all so wrong.
Your lips, your touch, your soft gentle ways
Take me back to all our yesterdays.

What is it you do to make me yearn?
For I feel not in control as my body burns.
I hunger for your passion, it ignites my soul,
Your kisses, your hugs, I just want it all.

But I gave it away, so many years before
Without stopping to think as I closed the door.
What we once had, was magical and true
And what I once had, my heart carved out for you.

I desire it now, yet my soul deserves to ache
And remember the pain of when your heart I did break.
A fantasy reunion for me is all that is left
And ironically now is it I, that feels bereft.

You have a place in my heart, that can never be erased.
Your name in my soul, that can never be changed.
A piece of my heart that still beats for you
And two lips that say I will always love you.

Little Seed In Me

How to explain to you now, just how I feel
The news has not sunk in, it just never will.
A seed growing inside me, will not see light
I hang my head in shame, as my conscience I fight.

I cannot ever entertain, the idea or thought
I could never give it, the love or support.
I have not planned for this, to ever happen to me
I just cannot accept, what will be will be.

I am tormented, between right and wrong
I am disgusted with what I've gone and done.
Is it my fear, or is it my self loathing?
My dreams I feel I am abandoning.

I have lost the ability to think so clear
I no longer wish to see those near and dear.
I want to turn my back and I want to run
No guessing what would happen, if I had a gun.

It's not just one life, I feel I am risking
But the lives of three, that will need adjusting.
I can't do this, I just can't contemplate
I just cannot leave this, all up to fate.

The noise in my head, is truly driving me crazy
What path am I going to choose, is really hazy.
When is it ever ok, to justify an abortion?
My head and my heart are in contortion.

Being a woman, it's hard to explain
I feel I carry the burden, the guilt and the shame.
No elation, no smiles, not once have I cheered.
I can't quite get past the hysterical tears.

I'm in a stable relationship, would it now cope?
I don't think so, I think it would choke.
I feel bad, I'm making the decision for us both
But I am certain if left, this child I would loathe.

It's just not in me, the timing is all wrong
To bring kids into this world, is a promise lifelong.
So what happens to me now, after decisions are made?
I will accept it's over, should you feel dismayed.

I pour my focus into thinking there's better days than this
And suffer in silence as the dark swallows me in the abyss.
You didn't ask for this, Little Seed to be
You certainly don't deserve; a terrible mother like me.

Not Ready To Be A Mum

I sit in sadness, with tears streaming down my face
Reality takes a bite, and puts me in my place.
I'm not ready to deal with being a Mum
I look at my belly, and dread what I've done.

I feel extremely alone, frightened and naive
I have to wonder what being "brave" did achieve?
I crave for the certainty, that no man can give
I long for the assurance of life to be lived.

I face the mountain, with thunder in my heart
I am at the bottom of it, and too afraid to start.
I know I should climb it, and deal with my fears
And yet, here I sit broken, my face wet with tears.

Too ashamed to ask for help & too weak to pull myself up
Oh yes, I've been here before, it's just my normal rut.
Feeling too guilty to believe I can be happy,
Feeling too pathetic to let it come naturally.

My husband doesn't see it, does any man really?
He can lock away feelings and just call you silly.
He can shoot you down, when you just want comfort
He has my heart in his hand, beating as loud as a trumpet.

I'm not ready for the next phase in life,
I'm not ready to become more than just a wife.
I'm not ready to deal with new changes it brings
I'm not ready to give up, so many things.

This poor creature, didn't ask to be born
This poor child, didn't ask for scorn.
This poor baby, created by us two
My darling Sproggy, what am I to do?

What will you make of me, when you are born?
I wonder if you will feel, just how much I am torn?
I can't say I will be the best mum or know what to do,
But sweet Sproggy, I'll always do what's best for you.

My Spark Of Life

Being a mum, wasn't something I knew I wanted
Until it meant being your mum, a role so daunted
My love for you darling, is hard to explain
As you give me so much pleasure mixed with pain

I watch you grow, and teach you things every day
I continually doubt myself, it is the right way.
You are my spark of life; I never knew I'd love
And sometimes I feel, so very unworthy of.

You are beautiful, sweet, wise, kind and fun
You are very much loved, by just about everyone.
I love you so much, my chest feels like it will burst
And to see you in pain, is just the worst.

Your teething, your tantrums, the separation anxiety
You won't remember most of these with any notoriety
They are my nemesis, and are just the worst
I don't know how to deal with them, they are a curse.

I have hopes for you that exceed the possible
But I'll help you get there, it's not mission impossible.
You are like a little blooming flower,
I treasure watching you grow, each day and every hour.

Final Decision

You know you have a best friend
When you class them as family
You were my sixth fur baby
And you gave us 10 of your years gladly.

I swear you would smile
When I would talk to you
And you looked sad also
When I said I had work to do.

You would sprint off excitedly
And dance at the back gate
Where you waited impatiently
For your other two legged mate.

You followed and ventured
And really just wanted to play
You enjoyed life to the max
You were fun to be with every day.

You loudly voiced your desire
For food and to come inside
And when there was a storm
You really just wanted to hide.

You were loved so deeply
And still are I must say
That I just couldn't believe
What the vet had to say.

My stomach flipped over
And my legs turned to lead
No way were you going anywhere
I couldn't accept it in my head.

I searched the internet intensely
So many positive diets and cures
I was going to prove them wrong
And beat this cancer of yours

I wouldn't give up on you
You would never have given up on me
You were far too precious and so loved
You were a big part of my family.

"Two weeks at best" we were advised
My heart was pounding, I was racing against time
And so cruelly it was not even two weeks
Your body started a steep decline.

My heart screamed "NO!" I could not lose you
My head said *do what's kind*
My world was boiling with emotion
I felt the final decision should be yours, not mine.

That last morning with you was glorious
We sang and laughed and had a party with you
We were celebrating your wonderful life
You just loved it and looked so happy too!

You ate off the table
At first a bit shy
But then you got into it
You didn't ask why.

Then it was time to drive, to the vet
It was simply agony for me
I kept looking at you and wondering
"should we just let you be?"

My final goodbye, I took off your collar
And gosh my hands they shook
I didn't want you to see my fear
I didn't want you to look.

But as the needle went in your arm
You glanced oh so briefly at me
I held you so tight against my chest
Only tears and sadness did you see.

You slipped away so quickly
My heart was banging against your chest
Now you will suffer no more
And peacefully you will rest.

Now you can play forever
And run and race and hide
You can't imagine the loss I feel
And the buckets of tears I've cried.

It's so sad at home now
I still look around for you
I know fur babies can't live forever
But in my heart they do!

Thankyou boy for giving us 10 years
Thankyou for being gentle and loving
Thankyou for choosing us
And thankyou for the kisses and hugging.

From Your Angel

I'm writing to you from Heaven,
I'm here now looking down at you from above
I can see you clutching my photo against your chest,
Your tears flowing with love.

Your grief is over whelming,
I never would have known
When I was alive and breathing,
Your love I was never shown.

I wanted your attention
And I wanted a nice warm cuddle
I wanted you to notice me
And I wanted to tell you about my trouble.

You would complain to your friends
That you never seemed to have enough time
You could talk for hours on the phone to them
And it was "hours" that should have been mine.

You were too busy with work
And too busy with life
You were too busy doing housework
And too busy being a wife.

You were too busy to sit with me
And too busy to seem interested
You were too busy to talk with me
And too busy to include me when people visited.

But here you are clutching my toys,
My works of art and smelling my clothes.
You are craving for my body warmth,
And to be tickling and playing with my toes.

I don't understand why you're doing this,
It's what I wanted always from you when I was there
You're looking at the card I was making,
At the time you didn't seem to care.

When I ran away from home,
I ran away to cry
I didn't know where I was going,
But I wasn't ready to die.

The nice man at the shop spoke to me
And stopped me crying with kind words
This complete stranger seemed so interested in ME,
I really felt I was being heard.

We talked for a long time, he bought me ice cream,
I told him all about you,
He listened to every word then smiled at me,
He had a plan about what I could do.

He wanted to drive me home
And tell you what a great kid I am
He wanted to tell you to notice me and love me
And for you to give a damn.

He made it sound so simple
I was convinced you would listen to his plan.
He was handsome and strong with a kind smile
And he was such a nice man.

So in his car I got,
I was smiling and happy and I was full of renewed hope
I had no idea I was not going to see you again,
I didn't even notice the rope.

You warned me about strangers,
But not really how bad they are
You told me not to talk to them
And definitely DO NOT get into their car.

I didn't think this was a stranger,
This was my new friend with a nice face
He listened to me so intently
And said my troubles he would replace.

He did things to me mum over and over,
Your name I did scream
You couldn't have saved me I know that,
This was a horrible dream.

So when Death came with arms wide open,
I gladly went with him
I knew you'd be so angry with me,
I knew my life would be grim.

So now here I write to you from Heaven,
And I'm sorry I didn't listen
I see your tears rolling down your cheeks,
In the darkness they do glisten.

You are talking aloud to me now,
Telling me how much you loved me
You should have told me sooner,
Because death we do not foresee.

There's a spot here in Heaven,
I'm keeping it safe for you
It's a seat right next to me,
For when your days on earth are through.

I think you will like Heaven,
No one seems to be in a rush
And when I get to see you again,
Your chest I just might crush.

Always In My Thoughts

There are certain times in my life,
I feel the need to question "why?"
None are more poignant than these two;
Who shall live and who shall die.

I know life is a journey we all have to take,
And "hard times" will make us stronger.
The pain will toughen us up to be more tolerant
And some days I really do have to wonder.

Why does it seem, more frequently than not
That the most loved people are taken too soon?
Yet despots, savages and the uncivilised
Live long lives and never will change their tune.

You were taken from us at the prime of your life
In a fashion that is too hard to bare
It's as though some misguided person thought
That you wouldn't be missed and no one would care.

It's almost like a bad movie script,
Catching planes and racing against time
To hopefully steal you back
And get to re-write your last lines.

Life seems so quiet and hollow now
I cry and I scream and it's into a void
The air seems sucked out from me
And life cannot be totally enjoyed.

For me, you are "missing in action"
I can't describe it in any other way
I haven't seen or spoke to you for such a long time
But I can recall your voice and hear what you say.

I feel as though I have been divided in two
Split open straight down the middle if you like
One half of me is so angry with you
Because you ignored me out of spite.

The other half of me is sobbing
She's totally all messed-up inside
She really just wants her daddy back
She feels so incredibly denied.

So I'm not the person you hoped for
I don't think I ever was meant to be
Our personalities warped and clashed
We were too much alike, you and me.

But, tell me this as I really need to know
If you lived your life over would you cut me out again?
Did you know just how deep the hurt you caused?
And tell me truthfully, did you ever feel the pain?

I'm not sure even I know the answer
To either question I pose
I just think there are things in life
And some chapters you need to close.

So wherever your spirit roams
North, South, East or West
I'm sure your love will guide you
To those that loved you best.

Second Mum

For 3 x years now, I feel I've become part of you
And you've played a really huge part, in my life too!
You embraced me as family; I loved your cuddles and kisses
I was so well looked after, and now I will miss this.

You've been there for my milestones, you've seen them all
From cutting new teeth, speaking, standing and walking tall.
I learnt sign language here, from such a young age
Your teaching skills are worth far more, than a basic wage.

You were my teacher, my mother, my friend and my rock
You gave me tools and the stage, for my brain to unlock.
You gave me your time, your patience, your love and your care
You've made my world just perfect, I will miss you not being there.

You are the perfect person, for a mother like mine
At home she was in turmoil, as all I did was whine.
You took me in and reassured my mum, I was in good hands
I blossomed and developed, and now she understands.

So it is goodbye to my friends, as a new chapter awaits
I'm sure if you check Facebook, mum will fill it with updates!!
I will never forget or stop loving you, for everything you've done
You're up high on my pedestal; I regard you as my second mum!

Grateful For Knowing You

When I first came to day care, you took me under your wing
I screamed, I cried, I vomited, over just about everything.
You cleaned me, fed me, loved me and settled me to sleep
You never shirked responsibility, even when it was knee deep.

Your endless patience with handprints, craft and creative ideas
My mum kept them all, and says it's the best she's seen in years.
You were there for me every morning, as mum handed me over
to you
You would nurture and comfort tirelessly, and that's just what you do.

Your strength is your unwavering dedication, to children like me
I know I pushed everyone's buttons, once I got older than 3!
You are open, honest, fair, a great adjudicator and more
You are everything any new mother, could ever hope for.

I will miss you heaps, and I will think of you lots,
I can already picture you welcoming, some new tiny tots.
I will forever be grateful for knowing you, at the start of my life
And I hope I can make you proud, by keeping out of strife.

Future Vision

On the day that you were born, I instantly became a mother
I didn't visualise it was a job, a position like no other.
Days rolled into weeks and the months they rolled into years
As I watched you grow up, it firmly cemented all my fears.

From baby to toddler, from tantrum throwing child to girl
You experienced most everything, but you were happy as well.
I anguished and worried, at some choices that you made,
As you moved from being dependent; to never being afraid.

You said it was true love, I rolled my eyes, I firmly disagreed
He was tattooed, spoke badly, I said he was not from our creed.
We fought fiercely and I forbade you, to continue seeing him
A shadow cast over your eyes, you bowed down to my whim.

And each new love you gingerly, brought through our front door
I told you he is just not good enough, don't bring him anymore.
Soon thereafter you changed and just stopped bringing the boys home
You said there was no point; I thought you preferred to be alone.

Then late one night for coffee, you brought home one of the best
"He's just perfect!" I gushed excitedly, "He's nothing like the rest".
He was tall and strong and gifted, and a gorgeous athletic type
He was handsome and cultured and I told you he was "Mr Right".

A wedding date was set, goodness you were such a beautiful bride
His family were sophistication plus, my heart it burst with pride.
As I hugged you on becoming a new wife, your eyes burned with hate
"Are YOU happy?" you said, "We need to talk, before it's too late".

"That's silly darling, why would getting married please me?"
"My whole life I only wanted the best for you, why can't you see?"
It occurred to me later in the night that we hadn't talked in years
I was too busy living your life for you, living it out of my fears.

We never ever had that talk; we never ever had that chat
I lost the opportunity forever and I sincerely regret that.
I am your mother, yes I love you, but I should have loved you more
I should have realised things are different, behind those closed doors.

I lost the right to know your dreams, I failed you my little girl
I lost the right to ask you now, and I lost so much more as well.
I wanted a life so perfect for you, a path so rich and true
I realise those things I wanted were for me, not perfect for you.

I realised so many things, some too painful to write
I realised I ruined your life, when I saw you one night.
You didn't see me staring at you, I was sitting too far away
I just watched you, thinking of what could I possibly say.

Where is your smile? Why don't you meet anyone's gaze?
Where is your confidence? It looks like it's been gone for days.
Your eyes and body language, looked tortured and broken my child
My arms lay like cement, yet your number I should have dialled.

Why didn't I move and rush to you? Why didn't I try?
Too afraid to face you or too afraid to see you cry?
I chiselled out your "perfect" life to fit the "perfect" mould
Reality is I broke your spirit and said "You do what you're told".

I saw your "true love" a while ago, I smiled, he excitedly said "Hi"
He's got a great job, loves life, has travelled the world wide.
He said he still loves you, and asked what are you doing now
I wanted to beg forgiveness, years ago I judged him badly and how.

Now more months have passed, the silence is all too loud
I've started to secretly follow you, in a large crowd.
I've overheard conversations; you have in coffee shops with friends
They tell you to leave him; you say 'No. The beatings they will end.'

You tell your friends you know; he's staying out at night too long.
And "No, he's definitely not cheating, he's Mr Right, not Mr Wrong".
You tell them that he's the best there is, your mother told you that
"She whipped all the Mr Wrongs off years ago, from her welcome mat".

You tell them that if it wasn't for me, your life it could be Hell
You could be married with kids to Mr Tattoo and speaking not so well.
This is the life your Mum wanted, perfectly written in her book.
You only marry for money and only a man who is a good look.

Your friends eventually stop trying, and soon they drift away
They might be gone, but I am still watching you, every single day.
Behind my rib cage, loudly beats my panic-stricken heart
I curse myself for wanting perfection for you, from the very start.

If I could turn back time to when you were born
And knowing what I know now, I'd silence all my scorn.
You'd make your own choices; you would succeed and fail
Be your own person, make mistakes, leave a heartache trail.

Success and failures teach us how to cope, with daily life
You would not have ended up being, a bruised and battered wife.
You could have soared with the eagles, laughed, danced with friends
Your life so full of excitement, and happiness that never ends.

You could have had all of this and more, that I haven't imagined
If only I kept my mouth shut, none of this would have happened.
I keep my distance behind you, having conversations in my mind
Motherhood is a treacherous job; it is one of a kind.

This is not the life I planned for you, my sweet darling girl
This is not the best there is, you are living a private Hell.
All the years I thought I knew best? I got it so wrong,
How on earth can I help you, I hate seeing this go on.

If I could re-run those years, would I push you into my mould?
Would I know what to do if I was you? I could I ever be told?
Can we start to fix this mess; can I call you for a long chat?
Let's meet up for coffee, so I can tell you "I've got your back".

How about I write to you and confess, I've watched you this week
Would you tell your friends, "Mum spies on me, but we never speak!"
What if I knock at your door, you open it wide, we smile and hug?
Then we sit down, laugh, have coffee and work on a latch hook rug?

Or how about I stop you in the street, instead of following behind
And tell you that you are a beautiful woman, you are one of a kind.
I'd ask you to look deep into the mirror, and what would you say
To your daughter, you'd tell her this life she's got, it's not ok.

Tell her love exists in hearts, but only those that are warm not cold
Tell her it's ok to raise voices, but fists they must be controlled.
Tell her to look at ugly paintings, for they hold the greatest joy
Tell her love is kind and overwhelming, and not discarded like a toy.

Tell her your wishes for her, are for her to be happy and free
And tell her to never listen to shallow people, just like me.
Tell her to be herself, explore it all to make her own path in life
And tell her only when she's ready, look forward to being a wife.

Most important you tell her you love her, in every sense of the way
Tell her mistakes were opportunities to break rules, you didn't obey.
Tell her you'll see her thru her journey, helping her when she needs
And tell her to never be a door mat, in a garden full of weeds.

For my child, read these words that I can't tell you to your face
I can only pray to God you find strength in them, to embrace.
You are my absolute joy; pride fills my heart when I say your name
I loved you and lost you, let's build your confidence again!

Teacher

You've been my constant, these past two years
When I've been naughty, happy and in tears
You've been there to support me, and guide me through
This maze called life, you're invaluable with what you do.

You are labelled a teacher, but really you are so much more
With your devotion and passion to us, we can really soar.
Imagination ignited in the classroom each day
We go home excited and not bored in any way.

We tell elaborate and intricate stories and fabricate some lies
And yet you treat us all equal, we see only love in your eyes.
When my mum drops me off, I'm not sad to see her go
Because I have you in my world, you are the star of my show.

The first year I pushed your buttons, boundaries and more
For that I am truly sorry, back then I was only 4!
Well this year I've given you attitude, back chat and lied
I'm so sorry about that too, my excuse is that I'm only 5.

Now here's the thing when kids are being so naughty so young
You get to blame it on their parents, because from them it comes.
I do tell my mum when I've been in trouble at school
And she tells me you were right; I have to follow the rule.

For she knows all about my moods and just how difficult I can be
And for this reason, she feels extremely bad to inflict you with me.
Your kindness, excitement and drive, to educate us well
She admires your commitment and is amazed you never yell.

You teach me about being at one with God, love and kindness too
I have these deep in my soul now, and next year I will miss you!
I've grown to love you these two years, so very deep and pure
I know I've not always been gracious about something so sure.

But please know Teacher, when I'm mature and school is done
I will remember the values you taught me, when I was very young.
People come and go, some leave "forever" memories along the way
But I will always cherish the ones of you, you've left me from Pre K.

Final Goodbye

Pushed to the absolute limit; I know I will break
Will you ever miss me, when my life I do take?
Your hurtful words, your spiteful ways
It's not worth starting again, I've had enough these days.

Don't tell me I am weak, because I choose suicide!
Don't tell me I should have spoken up, with the tears I cried.
Don't tell me, there was always an alternative to this
But look at yourself, how many cries of help did you miss?

So many times, I came to you with my head full of despair
You never quite got it, you never seemed to care.
It was too much for you, to see things from my side
Your resentment and anger, you did nothing to hide.

You shielded your emotions, as my soul searched yours for hope
All I needed from you was two strong arms to hold me so I could cope
I was sinking fast like I was drowning, and never quite got a breath
Before the next wave of black thoughts, crept in about death.

If only you'd shown me some compassion, or held me while I cried
If only you'd married someone else but me, I would never have died.
If only I picked myself up when you threw me to the floor
If only I packed my bags there and then, and headed out the door.

When I first met you, my heart exploded with surreal emotion
Nothing like I'd ever known in my life, I hung on every word spoken
Those days are so dim and distant, it as though they were dreams
You changed so much I don't why, our lives now pulled at the seams.

But ever the daydreamer, I hoped you would find your happy place
And we could once again enjoy the togetherness, in this rat race.
Fantasy websites, social media and other influences, interested you most
We were like magnets on the same pole, I could not pull you close.

So here we are once again living a lie, ignoring the problems in our face
I'm not the person for you, I'm not the person you want to embrace
You never want to talk about it, so the problem will never be resolved
So it's this goodbye from me, you got your wish, my life is dissolved.

How We Celebrate Easter

At Easter time, me and mum well… we do craft

For our friends and family and boy do they laugh.

Then I go on a hunt and find lots of eggs

I know they weren't there, when I went to bed.

Mum cooks a hot fruit bun, with a white cross

Then I tell my parents how Jesus died for us

I tell Mum & Dad, Jesus was buried in a tomb

He was wrapped in a shroud, in a very dark room.

Then I tell them how he rose from the grave

And how he told the angels our sins he forgave!

Then I tell them, that he sits at the right hand of God

And that he is my heavenly father and does a great job.

I Love You This Much

You were Peter Pan, never wanting to grow up or grow old
You were a cantankerous old git, who never could be told.
And conversations in general, when we got into it
Ended with your famous retort "well just don't quit!"

You loved your cigarettes, thin cigars and lawn
We all suffered with your emails, when the internet was born.
You loved your youthful looks and drank to excess,
At the end of all parties, you were usually a mess.

Your love of music, miming to the words, playing air guitar
You put all your effort into them, you were really quite the star.
Your endless energy to dance and shake your head around,
You acted out your fantasy, of an old rocker in town.

The long lectures of right and wrong, we endured as kids,
They went for hours on end, and listen we did.
You wrote the rules of how we should live by,
Yet you broke them all and I still don't understand why.

You could live and love others and forgive and move on
But not me, you let me know I continually got it wrong.
You loved strong women as long as they weren't me
Dad's aren't supposed to be like that, you'd probably disagree.

Seems pointless now, stating what is so obvious
Had you been a car, your care would have been meticulous.
You once told me you did not want to die with your body intact.
You wanted it well used and worn out, you accomplished that fact.

24 Hours Left To Live

I only had 24 hours left to live, but I didn't know it then
I had a fight with my parents and took off with my best friend.
I yelled and screamed at them, because they curbed my fun
I told them I was old enough to make plans, just like their son!

I only had 12 hours left to live, I was living the life
I didn't want to go home, I would have got into strife.
I was still a little angry, how dare they tell me 'no'
They didn't listen when I said, it was "THE" party to go.

I only had 6 hours left to live, I was ready to dance
We only had a few drinks, then I took a chance.
I got in the back seat, my friend he took the wheel
He was driving way too fast, I started to get ill.

These friends laughed at me, for being so scared
I realized true friends, should have really cared.
These friends didn't worry, if I felt secure
I realized these friends, were far too immature.

My countdown on life, had already begun
The wheels were in motion; it couldn't be undone.
I started to cry, no one wanted to listen
Tears fell from my face, I felt myself stiffen.

They stopped the car, with an ear-piercing screech
Then laughed and joked, about the speed they did reach.
The warning my Dad gave me, now I totally understand
"Don't mix with this crowd, because they don't give a damn".

I had my palm on the door, the handle was in my grip
I was getting out, putting an end to this crazy trip.
They all convinced me, to just stay in the car
They said they'd drop me home now, it was not too far.

5 hours left of life, an apology to Dad was on my lips
What happened next, was more like an apocalypse!
Another vehicle collided with us as we ripped off a U turn
We spun and flipped, then the car it started to burn.

My legs were trapped, but I felt lucky to be alive
It didn't seem that long, before help arrived.
The flames started to lick my back, I began to cry
I never thought for an instant, that I was going to die.

Panic rose in my throat, my pain was everywhere
I blacked out, it was really too much to bare.
The rescue crew released me, from my morbid tomb
Then I was rushed in haste, to the emergency room.

2 hours left to live, I think I knew it too
I know I should have listened, to my Dad's point of view.
My Dad held my hand, his eyes closed in prayer
My Mum was sobbing beside me, braced in the chair.

I wished I could have smiled at them, or just opened my eyes
I wished I could have said sorry, for going with those guys.
Instead I had to listen, to the heartbreak of their souls
They both said they'd give anything, to reverse these roles.

Now it's down to minutes, of my time left on earth
Ironic I should die here, in my place of birth.
I felt such strong love around me, now I know just how much
I loved my Dad holding me, I felt comfort from his touch.

My heart has now given out, my time here has come
My parents blame themselves, there's nothing they could have done.
They've paid THE price, for loving their child unconditionally
And Death just seems to take people, rather indiscriminately.

I'm desperately sorry, for not biding by their rules
And the awful things I said, words can be so cruel.
I look back and realise, they were just looking out for me
They always did, they always will, we were a strong family.

Blood On Your Hands

You have blood on your hands, from this very day
You have blood on your hands, that will never wash away.
You have blood on your hands, you spiteful little troll,
You have blood on your hands, thru to your soul.

Have I made it clear, that you are not loved?
Have I made it clear, that you betrayed your beloved?
Have I made it clear, that you will be cursed with pain?
Have I made it clear, that you are not welcome home again?

Your feinting, your sorrow, your great act of grief,
Proved to all who came, you are nothing but a thief.
You know what you done, you disgusting piece of trash,
No tears will be shed, when you are reduced to ash.

But not just me who wants to curse you with pain,
You brought great injustice to her and a world of shame.
And if you think she will welcome you home when you die,
You are sadly mistaken, for her true love with you did not lie.

The songs and the music, you foolishly thought were yours
Played so loudly at her farewell, were her choice of scores.
I laughed so hard and I wanted to shout out loud
"These are for her first love!", are you now so proud?

T'was The Night Before Xmas Ver 1

T'was the night before Xmas, Lyn was just getting to bed
Out of the corner of her eye, she saw a fat man all dressed in red.
"Who the hell is that?" she whispered loudly to Joel
"Someone is in our house! Could it be a troll?"

Joel got up to check it out, golf club in hand
Then he saw it was Santa, but very well-tanned!
Joel questioned why, as he stood in his pyjama's
"I had to make it up to the Misses, I took her to the Bahamas"

They laughed and chatted well into the night
Then Lyn stormed out, and turned on the light.
"Keep it down you two! Bryce is asleep!"
"If he wakes up and sees you, your balls I will keep!"

Santa turned to go, he was calling it a night
Lyn grabs him by the arm and said "hey! I sell Candle Brite!!"
"I've got mystery boxes, melts, candles and specials galore"
"Give these to your Misses, Santa. You will truly score!"

Santa's eye lit up, He handed Lyn his sack
"I'll take these to her now. Tomorrow I'll come back!"
Lyn screeched, "Don't leave your big red sack with me!"
"I've got Bingo at the Soccer Club, at quarter past three!"

With a hoot and holler, he slapped her on the arse
He high fived Joel, whistled a tune as he merrily walked past!
Lyn thought it wouldn't be too bad, she did look hot in red
Joel agreed and flipped a coin to see who would drive the sled?

The dogs were hitched to that sleigh, speed was not a problem
Lyn cried out "woo hoo" as Joel pinched her on the bottom.
She grabbed the sack and said to Joel "I've filled it with Candle Brite"
This was the year that changed Xmas, to every woman's delight!

T'was The Night Before Xmas Ver 2

T'was the night before Xmas, the girls had just got home
Getting the last of their Xmas shopping, at the Hyperdome.
Jode put her feet up, Tracy grabbed the wine
When outside they saw, a mysterious light shine.

"What on earth is that?" Tracy peered, thru the dark
"Some dude with a herd of cattle, this ain't no trailer park!"
"I'm going to sort him out and send him on his way" said Jode
So off she stormed, tired and fuming, barefoot across the road.

"Hey mate! You can't park these here" Jode said so terse
Once she realised who it was, she wished she could reverse.
"I'm sorry, I'm way off course and lost" the fat man said
"Rudolph ate magic mushrooms! The reindeers off his head!"

"Oh, come inside and grab a drink. You must feel quite drained"
"I'll just arrange some things" and to Tracy she quickly explained.
"We have to help Santa he needs a break, his GPS has died"
Tracy trembled "Thoughts of him when I was a kid, left me terrified"

In difficult times like these, someone has to bend
The way things start out, is no refection how they can end.
Soon Tracy was slapping Santa, and beating him at pool
Jode kept their glasses topped up, as Santa was pretty cool.

"Ok girls, I'd better dash, the sun is starting to rise"
"My cover will be blown soon, I'll have to go in disguise"
So off he drove, in Jode's car, elf dust in the tank
He sped thru his route unnoticed, now he had the girls to thank.

Rudolph was coming off his high, he looked pretty sick
Tracy gave him a scolding, no more mushrooms would he lick.
The girls looked after the deers, from neighbours they had to hide.
It was getting to a point, where it was pretty cramped inside.

Finally Santa did return, looking a bit worse for wear
His cheek was smeared with lipstick, the girls they did glare.
Jode roared "Give me my keys Santa, and take your smelly deer"
"Make sure you buy a new GPS, so you don't get lost next year!"

T'was The Night Before Xmas Ver 3

T'was the night before Xmas, Mark was in bed snoring
Louise was adamant, he'd be woken early in the morning.
As she plotted his demise, for keeping her awake
She heard a man shout "oh for Heaven's sake!"

Louise shot out of bed, fired up and sleep deprived
If she got hold of this trespasser, he would not survive.
So when she turned the light on, and adjusted her eyes
A fat bearded man was standing there, much to her surprise.

"Santa? Is that you? What on earth are you shouting for?"
"I left you the magic key, it fits our front door"
"Alright settle down, I merely grabbed the wrong one"
"I feel pretty stupid, but what's done is done."

"You're here now, come in, don't wake Mark"
"Get the sleigh off the lawn, the driveway you park"
As they sat and chatted, she said she didn't drink
Then laughed, said "Cheers" as the glasses did clink.

"You're lucky you know, your country is warm"
"I've been to terrible places, endured an ice storm"
"Oh don't get me started Santa, on places you go"
"This is your choice in life, no one forced you, you know!"

So police were called next, as the brawl did begin
The shouting and name calling, no one did win.
Poor Mark and family, had to hide from the public
Louise changed Xmas, it made them sick to their stomach.

Moral of the story, don't mix wine and no sleep
Don't whinge about your life, secrets you should keep.
Now Louise is serving time, plotting revenge and keeping score
Mark has to wash the sleigh, feed the reindeer and so much more!

T'was The Night Before Xmas Ver 4

T'was the night before xmas, Marie was watching TV
Binge watching Game of Thrones, season number 3.
All fired and feisty, she flouted her talent
She looked up at Tony and said he was gallant.

Their eyes locked, the moment did spark
When a hell of a noise, made Charlie bark.
Out by the letterbox, it sounded like 1000 mice
The expletives they heard next, weren't very nice.

They looked out the window, is that Santa on their lawn?
And all eight reindeer, seemed like they'd eat until dawn!
Santa looked up, said he was getting too old for this
He begged to come in, he was busting for a piss.

Marie looked bemused, can this really be true?
Is that really Santa, taking a whizz in our loo?
Tony called out, "Santa? Do you want a beer, mate?"
Santa replied "Yeah! Why not? The kids they can wait!"

So one hour of chatting, turned into two
Marie took selfies, it was a natural thing to do.
Santa thanked them for their company, he left with a sigh,
He gathered his reindeer together, and took to the sky.

Tony looked deep in thought, then an idea sprang to mind
"I'm going to race Reindeers? Do you think I'll get fined?"
"Sorry, Tony. I'm busy putting these on Facebook"
"Or should I wake Trudi first, so she can have a look??"

So Xmas changed forever, the tales did grow long
They'd stay up late every year, wondering what went wrong.
Santa never did come back, it was all too risky
Tony wondered if he should have offered him whisky?

He kept thinking, about a greyhound that could fly
How he could have hit the big time, was it still worth a try?
Marie disagrees with Tony, she doesn't dwell on the past
But she does wish she got an autograph, she just never asked.

T'was The Night Before Xmas Ver 5

T'was the night before Xmas, and Jack was awake
Shelly wasn't home, and it was getting late.
He heard a bang and a giggle, out on the road,
Shelly had been out drinking with Robbie and Jode.

Blowing a raspberry, Shelly came thru the door
She gave Jack a nudge, then fell to the floor.
"I'm OK!!" she said, "Wow, is that the time??"
"I swear last I looked, it was just after nine."

Their dogs start barking, at a noise in the yard
"What the heck is that?" says Jack now on guard.
A fat bearded face, stares in thru the glass
"that'd better be Santa, or I'll knock him on his arse!"

"I've got presents for Cameron!" the fat man blurts
"Wine for Shelly! Oh and Jack I got you shirts!"
"Come in then" Shelly slurred, "I need another drink"
As Santa squeezes thru the door, he gives Jack a wink.

"Well Santa, you can shove your shirts up your clacker"
"If you know me at all, my Torana needs a tracker"
"A new heavy duty tow bar, for my big blue Hilux"
"Foot pedals for the dirt bike, they only cost a few bucks".

"Whoa there Jack! You have quite a list to put in my sack"
"I haven't finished yet Santa! You'd better go and come back."
So off went Santa, the reindeers were rested and refuelled,
As he thought about Jack's toys, he pretty much drooled.

He got in his sled and uttered, "I don't want to be Santa Clause"
"I'm the one doing all the giving, this job is full of flaws"
"Imagine if I was hitched to Shelly? I'd have toys galore"
"She's a great catch, to let Jack bring them thru the door"

The house was abuzz Xmas morning, when the family awoke
Cameron ripped open his presents, Jack yelled "Is this a joke??"
Shelly not quite sober asked Jack to keep the noise down,
As he threw aside a box of wrapping, and sat with a frown.

"That sneaky Santa was going to come back with more"
"If I'd known he was lying, I'd have shown him the door!!"
"Instead he's left me instructions to drive his sleigh"
"He writes he's calling it quits, it's now his turn to play!"

'He's seen all my cars, boats, bikes and the van"
"He thinks he's missing out, living like a man"
"In our driveway, he parked his huge shiny sled"
"He says to keep it safe, locked up in a shed!"

From now on Xmas will be different, that's for sure,
The sleigh now has a V8, stereo and 4 on the floor.
Shelly fills Jack's sack with lots of Bourbon and wine,
Cruising the streets at Xmas shouting, "This sleigh is mine!"

T'was The Night Before Xmas Ver 6

T'was the night before Xmas, Elsa was drinking wine
Dean was watching TV, no one noticed the time.
A noise on the roof, gave them both a fright
Neither was game to look, at this hour of night.

Then a crash and thud, as something hit the ground
Elsa told Dean to go outside, and take a look around.
A sight to behold, Santa was on his arse
Elsa said "Just wait! I need a photograph!"

Santa said "I'm not so nimble on my feet"
"I knew I should have parked out on the street"
He gave Elsa a wink and handed her a gift,
Dean asked "Is it money for a face lift??"

They both yelled at Dean, at his attempt of a joke
"Come with me Elsa, you don't deserve this bloke"
"But Sinterklaas, where is it we shall go?"
"Elsa, I'll take you to a place full of snow"

"Ok, I'll grab a few bottles of wine"
"Don't wait up for me Dean, I'll be just fine"
With a crack of his whip, they were gone
"You'd better brace yourself Elsa, now hold on!"

They flew over land, Elsa could see snow
"Is it down there? That we will go?"
"I know where we are!! Oh, this is just grand!!"
"This is my hometown! This is Holland!!"

She was so excited, she raced inside the house
"Wake up everyone, I'm here with Sinterklaas!!"
Her brother cried and cheered with glee
"What a nice surprise, to see all my family!"

She missed her Gemma and Dean too
Soon thereafter in the sleigh they flew.
Sinterklaas felt, he was a failure
For her wish was to be back in Australia.

"Hey, I've had a really marvellous time!"
"And I managed to drink all the wine"
"But it's in Australia I want to be"
"Because I love my little family"

Dean was waiting for her return
No more jokes, a lesson he did learn.
Elsa said "It was great to fly through the skies"
"But this is home, this is where my heart lies".

T'was The Night Before Xmas Ver 7

T'was the night before Xmas, Helen was having a hypo
She was dressed for bar duty, and still wanted to go.
"Tee Cee get me a chocolate, a biscuit or something just fine"
What she probably really wanted, was a glass of wine.

"Helen, I can't find anything, since you sorted the cupboards"
"It's now emptier, than old Mother Hubbards!"
"Tee Cee it's right there, follow the aroma"
"Give it to me quick, or I'll be in a coma"

So on went this argument, no one noticed the time
In the end Helen said "stuff it! Just give me the wine!"
She pulled out two glasses, then set the table for tea
When she heard a scrapping noise, out by the tree.

"Tee Cee is that you? Crashing about outside"
"Nope not me" he calmly replied.
She pulled back the blinds, and peered thru the glass
    She was greeted with the sight of Santa's big arse!

"Oh my Lord!" shrieked Helen, as she blushed red
"I think I've had too much wine, it's gone to my head"
Santa spun around, as soon as he heard
He recognised her voice, even though it was slurred.

"Helen it's me! It's been a long time"
"I dropped my pennies, can I borrow a dime?"
"You'd better come in, it's not safe out there"
She started to feel woozy, she needed a chair.

Santa spoke up, he adjusted his pants
He yelled at the Reindeer, to get out of the plants.
"Sorry Helen. I've gotten a bit, blown off course"
"I'm really not with it, she wants a divorce."

Tee Cee interrupted, Ukulele in hand
"This is my wife, Santa. Do you understand?"
"She's not a counsellor, she's got her own drama"
"If you want someone to listen, go to the Dalai Lama."

Of course that was it! That's who could fix it,
He walked out the door, fed the reindeers a biscuit.
He turned and said to Tee Cee "You've got a good wife"
"This is a great home, you've got a great life."

"How about looking after the deer and the sleigh?"
"I won't be gone very long, maybe only a day?"
Tee Cee said "no worries. You can leave it with me"
Helen snapped "with him what did you just agree?"

"We leave in three days, for a cruise to the South"
"Don't believe anything, that comes out of his mouth!"
"He won't come back, he does what he likes"
"What are we supposed to do, with all these kids bikes?"

Not only did Santa leave his deer and his sleigh
He left all the presents piled up in the doorway.
So Helen and Tee Cee, they hitched up the sled
And distributed the gifts, both wearing red!

With a "ho ho ho" and a bottle of wine
They dropped off everything, in record time.
"Gee that was fun" Helen chimed with a smile
Tee Cee winked and said "I think we'll keep this a while."

T'was The Night Before Xmas Ver 8

T'was the night before Xmas, Thelma was in pain
She'd had more skin cancers cut out again.
JD was in bed and had just hit the pillow
When they both spied movement, underneath the willow.

"Who is that sneaking about, this time of night?"
"I'm in no condition, I tell ya, to put up a fight!"
"JD, please check it out, before you go to sleep"
"Or your presents under the tree, will be mine to keep!"

JD snuck a peak, then he pulled back the curtain,
At first he wasn't sure, but now he was certain.
"Hey Thelma! It's Santa. He's torn a big hole in his pants"
"That's why he's creeping around, in and out our plants".

JD calls out "Hey Big Fella! You'd better come inside"
"Thelma will sew up your pants, so you won't have to hide".
Santa's eye's twinkled, he knew Thelma couldn't sew
What could be worse, than his undies out on show?

He whipped off his pants, Thelma averted her eyes
And there she sat sewing, much to her surprise.
The magic in his pants, made her fingers fly
She nailed this sewing lark, and didn't question why.

Santa was ever so grateful, for what she had done
He knew how to help her, for getting too much sun.
With a twinkle, he left a special gift under their tree
He had to get going, it was nearly twelve thirty.

It was late on Xmas morning, when JD and Thelma awoke
They saw a gift marked "Love Santa", was this a joke?
It was "miracle cream" and Thelma howled with laughter
This truly was Xmas, this is exactly what she was after!

"Dab it on your skin, your sores will be erased"
"Next time you see your Dr, he will be amazed!"
"Unfortunately, skin cancer is a lesson you learn"
"You desperately wanted to tan, instead you got sun burn"

Thelma was so excited, she danced with Robin her cat
She didn't see JD's boots, sitting on the mat.
She tripped and face planted, straight into the floor
Now she has more problems, than she ever did before!

T'was The Night Before Xmas – Ver 9

T'was the night before Xmas, Ry was finally asleep
Shawn and Stacey then flopped in a heap!
"What a great day, Ry had with Steve and Jode"
"They had him mesmerised, with that Morse code"

Ry started to dream, he twitched and he wriggled
He was playing with Buzz, he started to giggle.
Grandma was in the kitchen, making some bread
She had lots to prepare, for tomorrow's big spread.

A cough and a splutter, made her call out to Shawn
"I think you'd better come see, who's on your lawn"
The family they stood, wide eyed and agog
It was Santa they could see, patting a dog.

"I've got presents for Ry and Lanie too"
"Can I come in, or shall I leave them with you?"
"Sure! Come in, but please don't wake Ry"
Oh no, it was too late! He had started to cry.

"Please bring him to me, I've not seen him for a while"
"They grow up so fast" Santa said with a smile.
Ry rubbed his eyes, yawned, said "Santa is that you?"
"You came to visit me, now that I'm two?"

"Hello there Ry! I brought you some toys"
"But I only bring them, to good girls and boys"
"We'll I've been mostly good, just ask Mum later"
"Yesterday she had to confiscate, my Tow Mater!"

"I know you've been good, it's here on my list"
"I brought you a new Buzz Lightyear, his arms you can twist"
Ry looked at Santa, the happiness burst from inside
He buried his head into his beard, thanked him and cried.

"Well I'd better go now Ry. It's been great seeing you"
"Be good for your parents and good for Grandma too!"
Ry waved him goodbye, with his new Buzz in his grip
"See you next year Santa!! Have a safe trip!!"

T'was The Night Before Xmas - Ver 10

T'was the night before Xmas, Donna was awake
She was putting pork in the oven, to slowly bake.
When a ruckus outside, stopped her in her tracks
Always the way, when she's about to relax.

She peered out her window, Roland came to her side
And listened to Santa yelling, that it was not a joyride.
He seemed quite upset, with his reindeer team
The noise woke Brant up, "am I having a dream?"

"Hey Jordan and Ethan, you've got to see this!"
"Old Santa's hobbling, he's got a slipped disc!"
They opened the door and went into the yard
Bindi was not happy, her teeth they were barred.

"Hi Wilkin family, sorry to make such noise"
"I've hurt my back. Could you carry these toys?"
They bustled him inside, for they really wanted to look
What was inside that sack? Donna hoped for a book!

The excitement roared as Roland spied a rod
Ethan held back, until Santa gave him a nod.
Storm and Sea Eagles!! The boys were over joyed
Roller blades for Jordan? She was slightly annoyed.

"Oh, they are for me" Santa said with a smile
"I used to be an expert, but it's been quite a while."
"This ticket is for you, you shouldn't think it's worthless"
"I bought another one, this one's for Curtis!"

Off into the night, Santa flew in his sleigh
They didn't want him to go, they'd love him to stay.
"How great he found us, now we've moved to the Coast"
"Let's raise our glasses to Santa, and to Santa we toast."

T'was The Night Before Xmas – Ver 11

T'was the night before Xmas, the Buff family all soundly asleep,
When Dick said loudly, "Can't you hear those damn sheep??"
Trev groaned, rolled over and opened one eye
"Aw Dick, it's nothing. Just look at the time?"

As Dick lay there wondering, what was making them bleat,
The rest of the animals began fussing, he got to his feet.
He looked down the paddock, couldn't see anything there,
He glanced behind the chook shed, Wait! Is that a bear??

"Get up! Get up! Trev, a bear is on the loose!!"
"Aw Dick, it's nothing. Stop acting the goose."
He pulled his face close, and gritted his teeth,
"You will go and find out, and give me relief!"

Trev armed himself wisely, with a torch and a hat,
He had no intention of doing, any more than that.
As he neared the chook shed, he let out a scream,
Is that Santa and eight reindeer? Surely this is a dream.

Dick heard Trev scream, he ran to the kids in their beds.
"Don't fret my darlin's, Trev probably walked thru some webs"
Then they all heard the sound of a big booming laugh,
Then saw the bright flash, like someone taking a photograph?

Heavy footsteps approaching, to their front door.
It was Trev and Santa, he'd been here before.
"Hello Dick, Bec, Maria, Chris and Trent"
"I crash landed the sleigh, it's got a big dent!"

"G'day Santa!" They chimed in as one,
"Can we ride your sleigh? I bet it's quite fun?"
Santa chuckled and called the kids near,
"Yes you can kids, but don't frighten the deer!"

They ran down the paddocks, to be the first to the sleigh,
Trev wasn't too far behind, and Dick was on his way.
With a chortle and chuckle, Santa sat on a chair,
As he watched the Buff's, get the sleigh in the air.

He got himself comfy, and promptly fell asleep,
When the sound of bleating, came from the sheep!
The Buff's had returned, boy they had fun.
Santa did a headcount, they hadn't lost anyone.

"That's it Buff's, it's time for me to fly"
"I've got to get these Reindeer, back in the sky"
Then quick as a fox, he was gone in the night,
Not bad for a fat man, on his feet he was light.

Next time Dick, heard a noise before dawn,
He rolled over and ignored it and let out a yawn.
Last time He heard something, he thought it was a bear
It's probably the Easter Bunny this time, he didn't really care.

Printed in the United States
By Bookmasters